GOD'S MESSAGE *to the* WORLD

GOD'S MESSAGE *to the* WORLD

You've Got Me All Wrong

Neale Donald Walsch

JAICO PUBLISHING HOUSE

Ahmedabad Bangalore Chennai
Delhi Hyderabad Kolkata Mumbai

Published by Jaico Publishing House
A-2 Jash Chambers, 7-A Sir Phirozshah Mehta Road
Fort, Mumbai - 400 001
jaicopub@jaicobooks.com
www.jaicobooks.com

Published in arrangement with
Rainbow Ridge Books, LLC
140 Rainbow Ridge Road
Faber, Virginia 22938
434-361-1723

To be sold only in India, Bangladesh, Bhutan,
Pakistan, Nepal, Sri Lanka and the Maldives.

GOD'S MESSAGE TO THE WORLD
ISBN 978-81-8495-794-5

First Jaico Impression: 2015

Printed by
Trinity Academy For Corporate Training Limited, Mumbai

To every sincere seeker.

Contents

The Basis of So Much

It's not a small thing to be wrong about God.

And if nearly everyone on the planet is wrong about God, it's *really* not a small thing.

If nearly everyone on the planet has mistaken notions about God, then nearly everything that everyone on the planet is doing will not work the way it was intended. This is because the basis of so much of what they're doing is found in so many of their beliefs about God.

Think not?

Think again.

Nearly all of civilization's modern laws emerged from the early rules and laws of some faith tradition. Nearly all of humanity's moral codes derive from the mandates of a religion. Nearly every political movement and economic theory is based on ideas of justice, right-and-wrong, and basic fairness first espoused by spiritual teachers.

Even those who don't believe in God are impacted and guided by many of the fundamental principles placed into the Cultural Story by those who do.

And a striking number of the personal decisions made by billions of individuals across the globe are made within the context of what they believe to be the purpose of life, what they believe happens when this life is over, what they believe about God, and about what God wants.

So it's not a small thing to be wrong about God.

☀

Proposition: Not one of the systems we have put into place to make life better on this planet is working.

Wait. It's worse.

Not only have the systems we have put into place failed to produce the outcomes for which they were intended—they are actually producing *exactly the opposite.*

I have made this point before, in previous books. I believe it is worth repeating, with emphasis.

Our political systems are actually *increasing* disagreement and disarray. Our economic systems are actually *increasing* poverty and the gulf between the rich and the poor. Our ecological systems are actually *increasing* environmental degradation.

Our health care systems are actually *increasing* inequality of access to modern medicines and health care services. Our educational systems are actually *increasing* the knowledge gap. Our social systems are actually *increasing* disparity, disharmony, and injustice.

And, perhaps saddest of all, our spiritual systems are actually *increasing* righteousness, intolerance, anger, hatred, violence, and war.

If the improvement of human life upon the earth were a laboratory experiment, it would have long ago been considered an abject failure.

Indeed, an appalling disaster.

*

Not everyone agrees. There are those who believe that humanity is evolving to higher and higher levels of sophistication and achievement, producing a better and better quality of life for all the members of our species.

It is possible that they would not, however, be among the 842 million people (one in eight in the world) who do not have enough to eat. It is certain that they would not be the parents of the over 650 children who die of starvation every hour.

They would presumably not be among the 20.9 million women and children who are bought and sold into commercial sexual servitude every year.

They would also, one imagines, not be among the over three billion people who live on less than $2.50 a day, or the billions who have no access to health care. (Some 19,000 children die each day from preventable health issues, such as malaria, diarrhea, and pneumonia.)

They would probably also not be among the 1.7 billion people who lack clean water, or the 2.6 billion without basic sanitation, or the 1.6 billion people—a quarter of humanity—who live without electricity.

That's right. In the first quarter of the twenty-first century, *2.6 billion people live without toilets, and 1.6 billion without electricity.*

How is this possible?, you might ask. And that is a very good question.

It is an especially good question given that humanity imagines itself to be a "civilized" species. To the people in the above categories, the "civilization of Civilization" has not even begun.

A planet where 5 percent of the population owns or controls 95 percent of the wealth and resources—and where most of that 5 percent think this is perfectly okay, even as unconscionable numbers languish in lack and suffering—would not seem to be a planet on which a great deal of humanitarian advancement has been achieved.

All of this is possible because of the collective values of those people who can do something about it. And where do those values come from? I suggest they derive in large part from the well-intentioned, but mistaken, beliefs about God held by many human beings—including those who do not believe in God at all.

Does anybody care that our species has been such a failure—or why?

Does anybody imagine it has *not* been?

Does anybody want to know how this whole situation can be turned around in the blink of an eye?

Does anyone want to know how his or her own personal life can be changed for the better with the embracing of a single idea?

Do *you?* Do you want to know?

Are You Ready for the Great *What If*?

IF YOU WERE THINKING this was going to be a once-over-easy book, you were mistaken. If, on the other hand, you are up to an intriguing, often controversial intellectual and spiritual challenge, you've come to just the right place.

More than that, this could also be one of the most important books you have ever read. For the world, it is intended to be exactly that: One of the most important books ever read.

If that sounds pretentious, I'm sorry. But it's a time for bold statements. God knows, it's time.

This book explores seventeen statements about God. Here they are:

- God is to be feared.
- God may not even exist.
- God exists and is a superhuman male being.
- God demands obedience.
- God sees us as imperfect, and we may not return to God in an imperfect state.

- God requires us to believe in God, and to worship God in a specific way.
- God is vengeful and God's love can turn to wrath.
- God was at war with the Devil, and that's how this all began.
- God determines what is right and wrong.
- God's forgiveness is required for us to get into heaven.
- God has a plan for us.
- God is on our side.
- God honors self-sacrifice, long-suffering (preferably in silence), and martyrdom.
- God sometimes answers our prayers and sometimes does not.
- God will reward us or punish us on Judgment Day.
- God wants us to return to heaven.
- God is separate from us.

Not one of these statements is true.

True or not, these statements epitomize what the largest number of people in our world who believe there *is* a God, believe *about* God.

This book challenges those beliefs. On these pages we're going to deeply examine The Great *What If?*

What if even half of the above statements are not true? What if a third of them are not? What if only *one* of them turns out to be mistaken?

Here's what's so: If even one of the seventeen statements about God above is not true, the whole list crumbles. The world's dogma about Deity falls apart. Because one depends upon the other for the whole dogma to hold together.

Yet the purpose of this book is not to dismantle anyone's belief in God, but just the opposite. The purpose of this book is to recreate that belief, to make it bigger and better than ever—by revealing a God who is bigger and better than most people ever imagined.

It will be no surprise, then, that some of the things that will be said here may take you to the edge of your comfort zone. They certainly will stretch believability.

If they were instantly, totally believable, *people would be believing them now.* Most people do not believe them now for a remarkably sad reason: They're too good to be true.

Yet if beliefs about *God* cannot be too good to be true, *what can?*

Still, I totally understand if you find it a little unnerving to enter into an exploration about God that moves outside the boundaries you are used to. Yet it shouldn't be a discomforting or disquieting experience to explore our understandings about God.

Nor should it be one that produces anger. Even if this book does nothing else but confirm your own present beliefs about God, it will have done exactly what it was intended to do. You see that, don't you? The point of the book is to point you to your innermost truth—and invite you to live it more profoundly.

The book simply opens the question. It simply engages the discussion. It invites a very personal examination by you of what you believe. To that end, it can't fail—unless *you* fail to engage it with a deep purity in your heart, a deep desire to undertake what could be, as I said, the most important personal exploration of your life.

*

God *invites* you to question. God *invites* you to wonder. God *invites* you to come to your own conclusions, not blindly accept the conclusions of others. This is bravery, not blasphemy. And the last I heard, God does not punish bravery.

What should be alarming to us is *not* exploring our understandings—ever. This can do more than simply bring our personal and spiritual growth to a halt. If millions of us decided to "stay put"—if millions of us simply refused to even explore or investigate ideas and beliefs about God other than those we have always adopted—that wouldn't be good for our species.

Millions of us *have* decided to "stay put."

That hasn't been good for our species.

In fact, it's one of the main reasons that such dismal conditions exist on our planet, and that huge numbers of people are unhappy—including many of those who are supposedly living the "good life."

When even people who you would think have *every reason to be happy* are not happy, *you know something's amiss.* And you know the problem must be *systemic*, or such a huge number of people would not be unhappy such a huge amount of the time.

That shouldn't be. That doesn't make sense. On a planet as blessed as ours, with a species as intelligent and innovative and inventive as ours, that shouldn't be happening. Something is not adding up.

So here's a question for all of us to ponder:

Is it possible that there is something
we don't fully understand about God,
the understanding of which
could change everything?

What Humans Simply Refuse to Do

THE QUESTION CLOSING THE last chapter is the first of a list of challenging questions you're going to find here. And this first question is the one thing that humanity is most not ready to hear.

We seem to be not ready to accept—indeed, to be *incapable* of accepting—that there is *even a possibility* we might have been wrong about *anything* regarding God.

I invite you now to observe something.

Not a small something. A *big* something.

Observe that humanity has been strikingly unwilling to do in one major area of life what it has been only too happy to do in every other arena of earthly experience.

It has done it in science. Happily it has done so, and it has produced extraordinary discoveries because of it.

It has done it in medicine. Happily it has done so, and it has produced astonishing miracles because of it.

It has done it in technology. Happily it has done so, and it has produced breathtaking advances because of it.

It has not done it in the arena of beliefs. Especially, beliefs about God.

Because humanity has done this particular thing in all those other areas, our species has indeed made some wonderful progress at improving life's potential and life's joy. Yet this progress has reached only the smallest percentage of our world's people (billions of whom to this day, let us remember, do not have the simplest convenience of electricity or the simplest dignity of toilets). The limit of this reach is the result of humanity *not* doing this one thing in the most important area of human experience.

And what is it that we have stubbornly refused to do in this single, critical arena that we have been willing and even eager to do in every other area of human endeavor?

Question the Prior Assumption.

In science, no sooner do we make a discovery than we question it up one side and down the other. In medicine, no sooner do we find a cure than we question every assumption on which the cure is based. In technology, no sooner do we create a new and wondrous application than we question its value, putting it to the test, making it prove itself.

In every one of these areas, the moment we decide that a conclusion we have reached is "right," we *question the Prior Assumption.*

Yet in the area of our beliefs, we do no such thing. Indeed, we do exactly the opposite. We say that to question the Prior Assumption is blasphemy, apostasy, heresy. The result is that we are moving deeply into the twenty-first century with the majority of us still devoted to and operating from ideas, beliefs, and conclusions about God from the first century—and before.

If we did this in medicine, we'd be performing surgery today with a very sharp stone.

Most People Agree: *God Talks to Us*

Before we go any further, you should know where all of this is coming from.

I am the author of the *Conversations with God* series of books. It is in those dialogues that I received the information I am going to share with you here.

Now you may feel that my belief that I have actually had conversations with God is outlandish—to put it mildly. Yet *hardly anyone who believes in God takes issue with the assertion that God has talked directly to human beings.*

There seems to be very little controversy around this. In fact, the followers of virtually every major religion maintain that its doctrines are based on the teachings of someone who they believe to have communed directly with The Divine.

I agree with them.

I believe that God inspired Lao Tzu, invited a greater questioning of life in Buddha, spoke directly to Moses, revealed divinity through Jesus, explained great secrets of life to Muhammad, whispered profound truths to Bahá'u'lláh, communicated through an angel to Joseph Smith, and has spoken to a long list of others not mentioned here.

Nor is this list limited to men. Humanity's historically male-oriented point of view has caused us to take the largest notice of, and to give the most serious attention to, the words of these and other so-called Holy Men, yet many women, too, have heard the voice of God and shared divine revelation with humanity.

Among them are Saint Elizabeth, Mother Mary, Melania the Elder, Hildegard of Bingen, Teresa of Avila, and Joan of Arc. And more contemporarily, H.P. Blavatsky, Annie Besant, Mother Teresa, Mātā Amṛtānandamayī Devī, and Mother Meera. This list, as well, includes many names not found here.

Now I do not consider myself to be on a par with those individuals. Not in terms of the impact they have had, and continue to have, on the human family—and certainly not in terms of their personal spiritual development. But I do consider myself—even as I consider every human being who has ever lived, lives now, and ever will live—to be equal with those listed above in terms of worthiness to be spoken to by God.

I'll go further. I know that all of us *are* being spoken to. Every minute, every hour, every day.

What's going on is that we simply call God's communications something else. Serendipity . . . coincidence . . . women's intuition . . . inspiration . . . a sudden insight . . . a flash of genius . . . divine intervention . . . providence . . . whatever we think we can get away with without being ridiculed, marginalized, or dismissed out of hand.

We're dismissed if we say that God talked to us *yesterday*, you see, because while we agree that God talked to human beings in the "old days," we aren't so ready to assert that God talks to people during *this* day and age.

Did God speak directly to Moses on the mountaintop? No question. Did God reveal the nature of divinity, and of humanity's true relationship to The Divine, to Bahá'u'lláh 200 years ago? Millions have no doubt of it. Did God speak directly to someone in Tuscaloosa, Alabama or Hamburg, Germany twenty-four hours ago? No. *For the vast majority of people, the answer would be no.*

Why? Because the vast majority of people are very unclear, to this day, about the true nature of divinity, the true relationship of God to human beings, the true reason and purpose for all of life, and the true identity, mission, and intention of the soul.

All that's going to end here. Everything is going to be made very clear.

The text in your hand is an extension of my *Conversations with God.* Although it is not presented in dialogue form, the content here was inspired by The Divine in exactly the same way as that earlier writing, and emerges from it.

If you have read one or more of the *CwG* books, what you'll find here is going to sound very familiar. It'll be different in the way it's being laid out, in the simple and very direct way it's being offered, but familiar in terms of concept and content.

And I'm betting that's going to be very okay with you.

Why? For two reasons.

First, you know that everywhere human beings have turned for the past several thousand years they have heard the same old Ancient Cultural Story—and that this is precisely why most of humanity sticks to it. It is *familiar*, and thus, it is *comfortable*—even though it has placed our entire species in an extremely *uncomfortable* situation. So it's clear to you that it is only through the use of *the same tool of repetition* that a New Cultural Story can also become comfortable, enabling it to then be adopted and embraced as part of the next step in humanity's evolution.

Second, the deep exploration of the most important elements of the New Cultural Story that is offered here is more than a mere echoing of previously offered articulations. It is a razor sharp *focusing* on a powerful singular message—a message that shakes, alters, corrects, and rebuilds the foundation upon which our global society has constructed its presently dysfunctional systems.

This powerful singular message?

We've misunderstood God.

☼

Perhaps you belong to a second category of people—those who have not read any of the *Conversations with God* books, but who have heard of them, and may have wondered what the attention they've been getting is all about.

(Seven of the nine titles have made the *New York Times* bestseller list, the books have sold in the millions, and they have been translated into thirty-seven languages.)

If you're in this group, you will experience that this text zeroes in on their most startling assertions and crystallizes the messages that have touched the lives of people all over the world in a wonderfully positive and deeply healing way.

Finally, if you are one of the largest group of people who form a third category, you will not have read any of the *Conversations with God* books, and have never heard of them.

If that is true, you will find what is to follow to be a crisp, fresh, provocative—and most important, much *needed*—look at a central aspect of humanity's experience: a spiritual expedition that could awaken you to remarkable new possibilities for your life . . . and yes, for your world.

Our Well-intended Mistakes

We did not intend that anyone would be damaged by our Ancient Cultural Story. Just the opposite was true. We intended that humanity would be enlightened. We were doing our best. Yet it is as the wonderful Maya Angelou told us: "When we know better, we do better." And now we know better.

We're older now. More mature. Still in the earliest stages of our youth as a species, to be sure, but at least out of the newborn stage. And so, people everywhere on the earth are now opening to new truths about God—which are not really new at all, but what God has been telling us all along, but now more fully comprehended by an awakening species.

Today not just one or two of us, not just a few people, but millions everywhere are hearing God's Original Message, rather than our Ancient Cultural Story *about* it.

That Original Message was given to humanity in the very earliest ponderings of the very earliest members of our species. It was shared by the wisest in our clan, the elders in our tribe, the seers and mystics in our midst. The Message has never stopped coming through, and it is coming through to humanity today more ubiquitously and more accurately than ever, as we have increased in our ability to receive it, to understand it, and to widely share it.

Not coincidentally, nearly all of today's more comprehensive interpretations of the Original Message contain matching observations, reach similar conclusions, and describe comparable realities.

This text you are holding condenses many of these conclusions, closing in on the cynosure of today's New Spirituality: the simple but startling acknowledgement that our Ancient Cultural Story *contained many inaccuracies.*

As a product of these errors, we have been deeply dysfunctional in how we've created life on this planet. But we are now ready to at least explore where we may not have gotten everything exactly right.

And God is helping us now. In these very days and times, God is helping us. As with the spiritual books of old, this is what the spiritual books of today are all about.

They are God's Original Message, interpreted. But not through the filter of humanity's Ancient Cultural Story. Rather, with a new lens. With a willingness to ask: Might there be a New Cultural Story awaiting our discovery? Could this be the story that was originally told, before it became distorted?

Might there be a story so radically different, so miraculously transforming, so marvelously close to God's Original Message that it took humanity's growing up just a little to even begin to comprehend its magnificence? *Might it be God who is continuing to send us the Original Message, and continuing to invite us to hear it and receive it over and over again through the millennia, each time with new and maturing ears?*

☀

Mind you, those last questions started with the word *might*.

Do we have the courage as a species to at least question the Prior Assumption?

God is telling us now that we have made some mistakes. That's it, plain and simple. And God is being specific about it. The list of our major misunderstandings about God has already been presented here. But don't be confused. These are not the assumptions that we refuse to question.

The Prior Assumption is this: *All we've been told and taught about God is perfectly accurate and absolutely, completely, correct.*

There have been no misunderstandings. Not one. Our teachers have spoken immutable truth.

It's not just Popes who many consider infallible, it's every spiritual teacher and every spiritual doctrine we have held dear for so long.

The assumption of each generation is that every teaching, dogma, tenet, principle, precept, maxim, canon, credo, and ideology of our particular group's favored messenger should be lived to the letter.

Why has it been so difficult for us to question this assumption?

Well . . . setting aside the challenge of twenty-one major religions existing in the world today (and, by best estimates, something near 4,200 religious groupings altogether) . . . we come face-to-face with a simple matter of personal need.

We need to have *faith* in *something*. We are a fragile species, and if we can't have faith in our self-created systems—our political, economic, educational, environmental, and social constructions—we need to at least be able to believe in what we have constructed around our Deity.

At least the vast majority of us do. At last count, nearly five billion of the world's people profess a belief in the existence of a Supreme Being or a Higher Power. Most people have been told that what they believe *about* that Higher Power is inviolable, never to be contradicted, infringed upon, or dishonored. Wavering in one's faith could lead to very unhappy consequences.

And so, we stick to our guns (literally) about our Prior Assumptions regarding God. Nothing can shake us from them.

There is another reason many of us do this. It has to do with our need to believe in not only what we have constructed, but in the people who told us how to construct it. We need and want to believe in our parents. And our ancestors. And theirs.

It has to do with tradition.

Culture and tradition.

To step outside of one's culture, to violate one's tradition, feels very much like a betrayal, too much like an abandonment, of all who have come before, and all that has produced our ancestral past. We need to have faith in this or, when all is said and done, *who are we?*

Are we to make ourselves up brand new with every succeeding generation? Are the preceding understandings and the teachings of our elders to mean nothing? Is *everything* these days "toss-out-able"?

These are fair questions, and any intelligent person with a decent respect for the past could be expected to ask them. Yet I was intrigued by a remark made in an interview of Dr. Bertrand Piccard in the May, 2014 issue of *Lufthansa* magazine.

Flipping through the pages of this in-flight publication while flying to Bucharest to present a spiritual renewal retreat, I found a fascinating story about Dr. Piccard, who was born into a family of scientists and explorers in 1958.

His grandfather, Auguste, became the first person to reach the stratosphere in a balloon in 1932. His father, Jacques, was the first to explore the depths of the Mariana Trench in a submarine in 1960. Bertrand went on to study medicine and practice psychiatry and psychotherapy. In 1999 he become the first person to circle the earth in a balloon. In other words, this man is a groundbreaker, a pioneer. That is what he has honored in his own background, in his own family history, in his own rich tradition.

Said Dr. Piccard in the interview:

> "I like talking to people who regard the world differently than I do . . . it's like a stretching exercise for my mind . . . Another thing I regularly practice is putting my convictions to the test. What if I'm wrong in what I assume, and the exact opposite is actually correct? How would that change my view of the world?"

Let's Just Admit It. We've Been Wrong Before.

COULD IT BE THAT OUR present assumptions about God are inaccurate, and that in some cases even the exact opposite is actually correct? Would that change our view of the world?

Has being *right* all these centuries done much good? Could questioning whether we may have been wrong do much harm?

Absent any willingness to put our assumptions to the test, we might as well declare our evolutionary progress ended right here. We're not going anywhere. Things are the way they are. That's the way they've always been and that's the way they'll always be.

Isn't the world flat? Isn't the earth the center of the universe, around which the sun and the stars revolve?

If—and only if—the human race has had enough of it dysfunctional stick-to-the-story-until-the-very-end behaviors (to say nothing of its vengeful and violent acting out), will it move forward in its examination of the causes of its own conduct.

The fact is that *beliefs* create behaviors, and what we believe is that we have a vengeful and violent God. A jealous

God. A God of wrath and retribution. "Vengeance is mine," sayeth the Lord.

Really? Well, apparently, yes. The Holy Bible itself recounts the killing of over two million people at the hand or the command of God.

Can this be true? Or could the Bible be "wrong" about this? For that matter, could the Bible be "wrong" about anything?

And could the Qu'ran? And what of the Bhagavad-Gita? What of the Torah, the Mishna, the Talmud?

Might there be error in the Rig Veda, the Brahmanas, the Upanishads? Are there mistaken notions in the Mahabharta, the Ramayana, the Puranas? What about the Tao-te Ching, the Buddha-Dharma, the Dhammapada, the Shih-chi, or the Pali Canon?

Are we to believe every single word in the Book of Mormon?

Not all of these sources speak of a violent God, but all speak of *larger truths*, and millions have been touched by what they have had to say. The point: we have believed, variously, the words in all of these holy scriptures, and—to ask a fair question again—where has it gotten us? Is it time to question the Prior Assumption?

Perhaps so.

☀

No, not perhaps. Absolutely.

But why? What if we *are* wrong about God? What difference would it make?

Would it matter in any practical way in our day-to-day lives? Could it really have an effect on an entire planet?

Of course it could.

And would.

But every thinking person must ask, first: How is it that if God has communicated God's truths directly to human beings as so many religions assert, the messages those human beings have shared are not identical? Why all the differences, some subtle and some very significant?

What is becoming more and more clear is that, while it was God who was *sending* these communications, it was humans who were *receiving* them. And it was other humans who were *interpreting* what they received.

To put this succinctly: While the Original Message has been clear, not all the messengers have been. Especially those who received the message from those who received the message. In other words, the *interpreters* of what the first messengers heard and shared.

This is not the interpreters' fault. It simply reflects the ability of all those within a species to whom the message is sent to understand it fully when it is first presented. This, in turn, would have to do with *when*, during the course of a species' evolution, the message was initially received.

In humanity's case, this was many thousands of years ago, and since then our species has evolved considerably—and so we have expanded in our ability to *understand* what the Original Message was telling us.

So let's just admit it: the very first interpretations of the very first message may not have been totally, absolutely, and completely accurate. And that is the point here. The assertion is not that religion, per se, has gotten it all wrong. The contention is that the information may simply be incomplete—and thus, not completely accurate.

Can we just admit that?

We are starting to. It's taken a long time, but we are starting to.

Example: On April 22, 2007, the Roman Catholic Church reversed its hundreds-year-old teaching on Limbo.

For hundreds of years the church taught that the souls of infants who die without being baptized would find themselves in a place called Limbo, where they would be eternally happy, but would be denied "the beatific vision." In other words, they would not be in the company or the presence of God.

Then in 2007, an advisory body to the church, known as the International Theological Commission, released a document entitled "The Hope of Salvation for Infants Who Die without Being Baptized." In that pronouncement—the publication of which was authorized by Pope Benedict XVI, indicating his approval of it—the commission said that the age-old interpretation of the Original Message surrounding the denial of an infant soul's direct entry into heaven may not be accurate after all.

The conclusion of the Catholic Church, in the words of the commission, "is that the many factors that we have considered . . . give serious theological and liturgical grounds for hope that un-baptized infants who die will be saved, and enjoy the beatific vision."

Then the church document offered an astonishing and hugely important admission:

"We emphasize that these are reasons for prayerful hope, rather than grounds for sure knowledge. *There is much that simply has not been revealed to us.*"

(Italics mine.)

That remarkable statement suggests that a body as august as the Most Holy Roman Catholic Church holds that, even as late at the twenty-first century, not everything about God has been disclosed. Meaning, presumably, that there is more to be revealed.

This is not a small announcement.

Example: In 1978, the Church of Jesus Christ of Latter-day Saints (the LDS Church, or Mormons) reversed its long-standing prohibition against ordaining black men to the priesthood.

Its refusal to do so for 130 years from its founding in 1849 was said to be based on its reading of scripture, which produced the view that black men and women had inherited the so-called "curse of Ham." This notion not only served to prohibit black men from being priests, it was grounds to forbid both black men and black women from taking *any part at all* in ceremonies in LDS temples.

It was a case of blacks not allowed in any Mormon Temple—which were nevertheless thought to be the sacred houses of God. Mormons once believed the supposedly relevant scripture passage occurs in the Book of Genesis and concerns Noah's drunkenness and the accompanying shameful act perpetrated by his son Ham, the father of Canaan.

The Wikipedia article on this subject goes on to say that "the controversies raised by this story regarding the nature of Ham's transgression, and the question of why Noah cursed Canaan when Ham had sinned, have been debated for over two thousand years. The story's original objective was to justify the subjection of the Canaanites to the Israelites, but in later centuries, the narrative was interpreted by some Jews, Christians, and Muslims as a curse of, and an explanation for, black skin, as well as slavery."

Whatever the case, in 1978 the church's First Presidency and the Twelve, led by Spencer W. Kimball, declared that they had *received a revelation* instructing them to reverse the racial restriction policy.

The ban on black priests was lifted in a statement known as "Official Declaration 2" based, it should be noted again for emphasis, on what the church insisted was *a revelation from God.* (Italics mine.)

That remarkable statement suggests that a body as august as the Church of Jesus Christ of Latter-day Saints holds that, even as late as the twenty-first century, not everything about God has been disclosed—and *revelations are now being received* by regular, normal human beings.

This is not a small announcement.

Wait a minute. Let's not just skim over that. Let's give it more than a once over lightly.

A *revelation from God* has been openly acknowledged by a worldwide religion as recently as 1978?

Yes.

A *major change in ancient doctrine* has been approved by the world's largest Christian church as recently as 2007?

Yes.

So then, direct revelation from God apparently did *not* occur only in ancient times—and did not *stop* then, either.

This brings up an interesting question. Is it possible that human beings are receiving revelations from God *even now?*

Yes.

But is revelation limited to presidents of churches and Popes? Have only a few human beings received revelations from God?

No.

⁂

Now comes A Great *What if . . .*

What if the number of people
who have had conversations with God
is unlimited?

What if the list includes
every human being who has ever lived,
is living now, and ever will live?

What if God is talking to everyone,
all the time? What if it's not a case of
to whom God is talking, but who's listening?

Could such a thing be true?

The very idea shakes the foundation of our present reality. Yet here is an interesting observation from Mother Meera:

"One common mistake is to think that one reality is *the* reality. You must always be prepared to leave one reality for a greater one."

Indeed.

☼

Let us be clear on one thing: all the messages that humanity has received about God, from the beginning of recorded history to this very day, have come through human beings.

Let us be so clear about this that we say it again, in capital letters.

All the messages that humanity has
received about God, from the beginning
of recorded history to this very day,
HAVE COME THROUGH HUMAN BEINGS.

God is revealing divinity to humanity *through h*umanity continually.

God has never stopped and God never will.

Humanity is now growing in its ability to hear God's revelations more clearly, and to interpret them more accurately.

This is a result of humanity's maturation as a species.

Now, after many thousands of years, we have advanced to the point where we are developing both an open mind and an open ear for the continuing revelations of The Divine.

We have grown to accept that receiving such revelations even today—not just in "the old days"—is possible, and we have expanded our ability to directly experience this as a reality.

It has helped that, while it has taken many, many generations to do so, we have finally begun distancing ourselves from unquestioning allegiance to the teachings of the past.

We are allowing ourselves to take what is good from those teachings and continue to apply it, but also to sift and sort what is dysfunctional, releasing ourselves, finally, from the limiting and psychologically damaging impact of many of those ancient interpretations of the Original Message.

Let's begin doing so at a new level.

Let's begin right now.

Our First Misunderstanding about God: *God is to be Feared*

Of all the things I've been told about God through all the years that I've been on the planet, the saddest thing I've ever heard is something that has been spoken over and over and over *again* by all the voices of authority: *Be afraid of God.*

Christianity is replete with such admonitions. So is Islam. So are the teachings of Judaism. From each of these major religions we hear words such as these . . .

> "Fear God, and keep his commandments: for this is the whole duty of man." (Ecclesiastes 12:13); "The fear of the Lord is the beginning of wisdom." (Proverbs 9:10); "And whoever fears Allah, he will make for him a way out." (Surah at Talaq 65:2); "Let all the earth fear the Lord." (Psalms 33:8)

There's more. Much more.

> "Let us cleanse ourselves from all filthiness of the flesh and spirit, perfecting holiness in the fear of God." (2 Corinthians 7:1)

Holiness is perfected through the fear of God? Yes, that's been the teaching. And it has been shared not just with the pious and holy few in monasteries and studious seclusion who have been seeking "holiness," but widely spoken, so that "all the people of the earth might know the hand of the Lord, that it [is] mighty: that ye might fear the Lord your God forever." (Joshua 4:24)

Now comes The Great *What If* . . .

What if we need not
fear God for any reason?

Would it make a difference? Does it matter? In the overall scheme of things, would it have any significant impact in our planetary experience?

Yes. Of course it would. If we thought that we had no reason to fear God, the bottom would drop out of most every religious doctrine in the world. Religion itself would not disappear (I do not think the idea and the practice of honoring our natural impulse toward The Divine will ever vanish from the human experience), but only its "high" would remain. Its bottom—the notion that God *must* be feared because God is an angry, judgmental, condemning, and punishing Deity—would dissolve.

Then, we would have to find another reason to act or not act in a certain way, do or not do a certain thing, hold or not hold a certain thought about life, about each other, about why we are here in physical form, and about the whole experience, top to bottom, of humanity's presence on this planet.

But it would take a lot to convince us that God is not to be feared. We've gotten the message. And in case we haven't, it's been repeated to us—taken from the scriptures and put into their own words—by many people we have reason to admire.

Like David Livingstone, a widely known and immensely popular national hero in Great Britain, whose meeting with H. M. Stanley in 1871 while working as a medical missionary in Africa gave rise to the popular quotation, "Dr. Livingstone, I presume?", and who told us: "Fear God and work hard."

Like Oswald Chambers, the early twentieth-century Scottish evangelist and teacher, best known as the author of the devotional, *My Utmost for His Highest*, who told us: "The remarkable thing about God is that when you fear God, you fear nothing else, whereas if you do not fear God, you fear everything else."

Like Ray Comfort, a present-day Christian minister and evangelist who wrote *The Way of the Master*, and who told us: "When men don't fear God, they give themselves to evil." (In other words, it's only fear of God that stops us from behaving badly.)

Or—not to put too fine a point on it, but—like Charles Inglis, an Irishman and the first bishop in the Church of England for the diocese of Nova Scotia in the early nineteenth century, who modeled what thousands of clergy have done before and since, perfectly echoing scripture when he told us: "To fear God is one of the first and greatest duties of his rational creatures."

So we see, then, that fearing God is a *duty.*

⁂

My childhood experience of Catholicism was that it is a really friendly religion. All I had to do was go to Mass on Sunday, go to Confession on Saturday, receive Holy Communion regularly, obey the Commandments, follow the teachings of the church, live a life as free of sin as possible, and I'd be good with God.

But if I seriously questioned what I was taught—and most certainly if I *rejected* any major aspect of it—God would not be happy with me, and there could be hell to pay.

Literally.

And my religion was not the only religion that historically put fear into the hearts of men and women.

Consider this announcement, made back in May of 1420:

> A Sudanese court has sentenced a pregnant 27-year-old woman, Meriam Yehya Ibrahim, to death for marrying a Christian man and affirming her faith in Christianity.
>
> The woman stands accused and convicted of apostasy, as the court in Khartoum regards her as a Muslim. The court considered immaterial the fact that she was raised Christian by her mother after her Muslim father left when she was six years old.
>
> Because her father was Muslim, the courts considered her one, too, making her marriage to a non-Muslim man not recognized and void. She has therefore also been convicted of adultery, and sentenced to 100 lashes.

I'm so sorry, I made a typo there. I typed those numbers in reverse order. That was not back in May, 1420—that was back in May, *2014*.

You read that right. In *2014* a woman was sentenced to *death* after being convicted of renunciation of her Islamic faith. Her conviction was overturned only after an international outcry. And so we see that between the fear of hell and the fear of death, religions have, to this day, found a way to keep the faithful . . . well . . .

. . . faithful.

Merely questioning official religious doctrine can result in being shunned or marginalized by one's spiritual community—to say nothing of, in some nations, facing formal charges of apostasy, resulting in expulsion from the country, or even a sentence of death.

On top of the anxiety and terror that has been instilled in the faithful (or should they be called "the fearful"?), there is that previously mentioned natural inclination in many people to never in any event doubt, question, or challenge their most deeply held beliefs, because they think that to do so would dishonor their family, tradition, or culture.

Put fear of God and reluctance to dishonor the past together and it's no wonder that spiritual exploration beyond the borders of accepted doctrine and adopted orthodoxy does not come easily to human beings. Yes, it *can* be deeply unsettling at best, and scary at worst.

Where does this age-old idea that we are supposed to fear God come from? It is based on the false notion that there are two things that God wants: Love and Justice.

We are told that to fulfill His first desire, God has granted each human being ample and repeated opportunity to be reconciled with Him. To fulfill the second, God, at the end of each human life, sits in judgment of every human soul, deciding at this "reckoning" whether the soul has earned everlasting reward in heaven or everlasting damnation in hell—or something in between: a possible sentence of temporary, but agonizing, "purification" in what Catholics and some other Christians call Purgatory.

(Members of the Church of Jesus Christ of Latter-day Saints refer to this not-eternally-damned place as Spirit Prison, where souls are said to exist in pain, guilt, and anguish, but only until the final judgment, when all are given another and last chance to declare that Jesus Christ is their savior.)

The reason for all this, we are told, is that nothing but perfection and holiness may exist in heaven. (We'll be talking more about this later.) Since few of us die in a state of absolute perfection and complete holiness, some of us must go to an interim location in order to be cleansed of our sins through torment and suffering that is hellish, but not eternal. The length of our suffering is apparently determined by the length of the list of our sins.

Others of us must go straight to hell, there to suffer forever for sins we've committed that are so serious, they cannot even be burned away through temporary torment; they simply cannot and will not be forgiven by God.

While Catholics speak of purgatory perhaps more than people of some other faiths, this notion of an interim (and fearful) experience prior to entering heaven is not limited to Catholicism, nor even to the broader category of all the sects in Christianity. The practice of caring for the dead and praying for them existed long before the birth of Christ—as, for instance, in certain Egyptian rites. It is found in Islamic and Judaic traditions as well.

Indeed, ancient holy scriptures speak of a process of *apocatastasis*—a term derived from the ancient Greek which is understood to mean reconstitution, restitution, or restoration to the original or primordial condition.

Human beings on the earth are said to be able to assist the souls of the dearly departed through prayers and offerings. In early Christianity the wealthy could be said to obtain for their deceased beloveds what was called a Plenary

Indulgence—springing them free from purgatory instantly upon the bestowing of a great sum of money, or lands, or both to the Catholic Church (which practice led to Martin Luther's decision to openly protest, resulting in the Protestant movement called The Reformation).

With all this worrying about, praying and caring for the dead having gone on for all these thousands of years, it is small wonder that so many people to this very day fear what God's wrath may impose on them after death.

GOD'S MESSAGE TO THE WORLD

God has been telling us from the very beginning, and it is becoming more clear to us every day, that **humanity's Ancient Cultural Story about needing to fear God is plainly and simply inaccurate.**

It is okay now to remove this ancient teaching from our current story, and to stop telling this to ourselves and to our children.

The *last* thing God would suggest is that we fear God.

God does not even command us to love God. We *can* love God if we want to, but God does not need us to, require us to, or command us to. Love is not something God commands. Love is what God *is*.

God experiences what God is whether we know it or not. God does not need us to supply to God what God is, in order for God to experience it. God supplies *us* with what God is, and the sadness is, we very often *refuse* to experience it.

What kind of a Deity would command us to fear God and to love God at the same time? This is the question you have to ask if you are going to fairly address the matter of whether this kind of theology makes sense.

The current theology of billions asserts that God is a jealous God, a vengeful God, and an angry God who uses violence on human beings and who has commanded human beings to do so on each other. It also declares that God is a caring God, a compassionate God, a merciful God, and a loving God who wants nothing but the best for us.

One result of this teaching: Even as most humans feel they have to fear God, they also want to love God. Many human beings thus confuse fear and love, seeing them as connected in some way.

Where God is concerned, we love to be afraid and we're afraid not to love. We've actually made it a *virtue* to be "God fearing," even as we seek to keep the commandment to *"Love the Lord thy God with all thy mind, all thy heart, and all thy soul."*

According to our Ancient Cultural Story, God has made it clear that He loves humans if they do what He wants. If they do not, humans shall know His wrath. They'll be condemned to everlasting damnation.

Some say that God acts with love when He shows His wrath. He takes kind of a "this hurts me more than it hurts you" parental profile. He is loving when He condemns people to eternal and unspeakable torture. With this explanation, they seek to preserve the image and the notion of a loving God.

Thus, many people have become very confused about the true nature of love. Human beings "get," at some deeply intuitive level, that the imposing of unending punishment does not seem like a very loving thing to do. Yet they are told that such punishment is a demonstration of the purest and highest love, with God simply seeking to preserve perfect justice and pure holiness in heaven. Since God is just, He must exact justice, so the ancient story goes. It's God's love in action (God's love of perfection, if not God's love of people).

This packaging of love and fear in human theology has not been without consequences in human behavior. People have become skittish about the very thing they want the most.

The notion that God must exact justice through punishment suggests that God is paralyzed by His own law, and has less freedom than a judge in a human court of law. God is simply unable to do as He says He chooses.

This would indeed give us cause to be fearful, for we have a God who apparently has no choice regarding His own decisions.

It's not unusual for human beings to therefore be afraid of human love, even as they have been made afraid of God's love. They have been taught that God's love can turn to wrath in a flicker, producing horrifying results—and that God has no choice about this. *"Dem's da rules."*

Or, worse yet, that God *does* have a choice about it, and actively chooses, every single time, without exception for mercy or compassion, to condemn souls to everlasting damnation, unrelenting torture, eternal anguish, and indescribable suffering in the fires of Hades.

Having had all of this made clear about their relationship with God, people often move into a closer love relationship with each other plagued by an understandable thought: "Now what is this person going to want, need, or expect from me? And how will I be punished if I don't supply it? Will I hear the answer to that question in Divorce Court, where I will be judged?"

This is, after all, our understanding of the nature of our relationship with an all-powerful God. Why or how would it be anything less with a much weaker fellow human being?

There is also the corollary thought that partners in a relationship have a *right* to expect certain things in exchange for love—even as God expects certain things—and that love is therefore a *quid pro quo* proposition.

These expectations and fears undermine many love relationships at the outset. They certainly undermine our relationship with God.

And there is another ramification of all of this. Because the highest love describable and the worst torture imaginable have been linked in the minds of humans as natural expressions on the part of God, most humans believe that it's right and proper for them, as well, to love and torture others at the same time—and to personally judge, condemn, and punish others who offend them.

This has created an entire system of what we have labeled "justice" in our world—much of which perpetrates, by almost everyone's most candid assessments, *in*justice far too often.

Let us be clear, now and forevermore, that fear of God is not the ideal or highest state of holiness, consciousness, spirituality, or even religiosity. It is, in fact, the furthest thing from it.

Let us make a point of that.

Fear of God is not the ideal or highest state of holiness, consciousness, spirituality, or even religiosity. It is, in fact, the furthest thing from it.

Fear of God must necessarily be based on a false thought. The thought is that God is going to "get" us if we don't do what God wants. Somewhere inside of us we know that this can't be true, and so fear of God feels the way a lie feels. Have you ever noticed how your stomach turns when you know you're telling a lie? That is how your stomach feels when someone tells you to fear God.

The sadness of most theologies is that they require us to adopt the notion that the joyous nature and the wondrous quality of both this life and the life hereafter is not a guarantee.

Embracing a fear of God is your declaration that God has a preference in the matter of how you live your life—and that God has no way of experiencing this preference without using on you the threat of retribution beyond your worst nightmare.

Fear is the logical outcome of humanity having accepted, as if they were true, five fallacies about God: First, that God *needs* something. Second, that God *can fail to get* what He needs. Third, that God *has separated* you from Him because you have not given Him what He needs. Fourth, that God still needs what He needs so badly that God now *requires* you, *from your separated position*, to give it to Him. Fifth, that God *will destroy you* if you do not meet His requirements.

Each of these statements would seem to be so obviously fallacious on their surface that they hardly deserve further discussion. Yet taken as a group, they comprise *the foundational basis of most of the world's religions*. And what is remarkable is that humanity has been unable to acknowledge that these five fallacies have brought more pain and destruction to day-to-day existence than all other beliefs about life combined.

The fact is that, as spiritual teacher Ernest Holmes wrote in his wonderful book, *The Science of Mind:*

> "Love is the central flame of the universe; nay, the very fire itself. It is written that God is Love, and

that we are His expressed likeness, the image of the Eternal Being.

"Love is self-givingness through creation, the impartation of The Divine through the human. Love is an essence, an atmosphere, which defies analysis, as does life itself. It is that which IS and cannot be explained: it is common to all people, to all animal life, and evident in the response of plants to those who love them. Love reigns supreme over all.

"The essence of love, while elusive, pervades everything, fires the heart, stimulates the emotions, renews the soul and proclaims the Spirit.

"Only love knows love, and love knows only love. Words cannot express its depths or meaning. A universal sense alone bears witness to the divine fact: God is Love and Love is God."

What is to fear in that?

Nothing. Absolutely nothing. Yet millions—nay, billions—continue to be enslaved by the thought that it is wise and good to be "God fearing."

What the world would grandly benefit from right now is a *civil rights movement for the soul*, freeing humanity at last from the oppression of its beliefs in a violent, angry, and vindictive God.

Another Misunderstanding about God: *God May Not Even Exist*

After the idea that God is to be feared, the second most damaging notion that some humans hold about God is the thought that God might not even exist.

Why this is damaging is that it stops all atheists and many agnostics from using God's power, even as the whole of humanity seeks to work collaboratively to create the life we all say we want for everyone on this planet.

If you see a sign on your front door from the city that the electricity is off in your house, you will not bother turning on a lamp, having concluded that there's no point in doing so. You will then be in the dark. The power that's flowing will be useless to you because you do not believe that it is flowing. You will not even test it, because you've been told *by someone in authority* that the power is out.

It is estimated that right now over 10 percent of the world population thinks that the power is out. That's roughly the number of people who categorize themselves as non-religious, with 2 percent actually declaring atheism. And of the vast majority who say that they *do* believe in God, an enormous number nevertheless have occasional—and sometimes lifelong—doubts about whether the God in whom they believe actually exists.

☀

Now comes The Great *What If*...

What if it is true, beyond
a shadow of a doubt,
that God exists?

Would it make a difference? Does it matter? In the overall scheme of things, would it have any significant impact in our planetary experience?

Yes. If the entire world believed without question that a Higher Power exists, out of which life on the earth emerged, it would create a universally accepted context, a sacred or theological basis, for humanity's collective formulation of fundamental values.

Right now the values guiding the behavior of our species are not collective or uniform. They are scattered all over the place.

One person may believe that abandoning one's religion should be punishable by death, while another person may believe that the person who *put* another person to death for abandoning a religion should be put to death—to use a glaring example brought up by the news account in Chapter 2.

One person may believe that the purpose of life is to live in such a way as to please God and get to heaven, while another person may believe that the purpose of life has nothing to do with pleasing God, even as a third person may believe that there is not even a God to please.

One person may believe that all souls who do not believe in the One True Religion are going to hell, while another person may believe that all souls who seek God with a desire pure and true will avoid going to hell, even as a third person may believe that there is not even a hell to go to, much less a God to send people there.

One person may believe good and evil are defined by God, while another person may believe that God does not view the actions, choices, and decisions of human beings in these terms, even as a third person may believe that there is no Deity at all to apply such labels to human behaviors.

One person may believe that killing people as a punishment for certain crimes, or even as a means of "defending the faith," is in accordance with God's Law, while another person may believe that killing people for any reason is not in any way in harmony with God's Law, even as a third person may believe that there is no such thing as God's Law, much less a God to announce it.

Without a common belief in the existence of a Deity and a shared understanding of what is true about and for that Deity, we can't even agree on a reason for living, the purpose of our existence, the experience—if any—that follows death, and the basis for life's largest decisions (both as an individual and as a society).

GOD'S MESSAGE TO THE WORLD

God has been telling us from the very beginning, and it is becoming more clear to us every day, that **the portions of humanity's Ancient Cultural Story which instill doubt about whether or not there even is a Higher Power in the universe are plainly and simply inaccurate.**

It is okay now to remove this ancient teaching from our current story, and to stop telling this to ourselves and to our children.

God exists.

Make no mistake about it.

God exists.

While there are those who feel that science and spirituality are the antithesis of each other, the greatest scientific mind of our time, Albert Einstein, said: "I believe in Spinoza's God, who reveals himself in the orderly harmony of what exists, not in a God who concerns himself with fates and actions of human beings."

It has been said that when he was asked by David Ben-Gurion (the primary founder and the first prime minister of Israel) whether he believed in God, Einstein—who, of course, uncovered and proposed a world-changing formula about energy and mass—agreed that *there must be something behind the energy.*

It might be worth, then, highlighting this:

Make no mistake about it.
God exists.

Albert Einstein also said, "I cannot imagine a God who rewards and punishes the objects of his creation, whose purposes are modeled after our own—a God, in short, who is but a reflection of human frailty."

Is this something upon which we can agree? God was not made in the image and likeness of Man.

Who or what, then, *is* God?

Here is an analogy that may help us answer this ancient question.

As humanity has moved more deeply into the twenty-first century, medical science has learned more and more about what it has called "stem cells." These are described as undifferentiated biological cells that can differentiate into specialized cells, and can divide to produce more cells of a specialized kind.

If harvested from a human body before they differentiate, they can be "coaxed" in a laboratory into adopting the specialized identity of *any cell in the human body.* This means that they can regenerate any portion of virtually any organ of the body—from brain cells to lung tissue to heart muscle to the follicles of hair on your head. This has led to a whole new branch of medicine emerging under the loose heading of nanobiotechnology.

The point of bringing all this up here?

If "nature" can do all of this within the vastly limited framework of a single human body, what could one drop of the Primal Force or the Essential Essence do within the unlimited framework of the cosmos?

Are human stem cells showing us something on the micro level that tells us something about life on a macro scale? Could God be, in a sense, *the stem cell of the universe*, able to differentiate in any one of countless ways?

Consider this: Cosmologists are now telling us that our universe may be—and probably is—just one of an *infinite number* of such manifestations. In other words, as unfathomably large as we have assumed our universe to be, it may be merely a spec in a universe of universes.

Or, to put it another way, we may live not in a *uni*verse, but in a *multi*verse.

This would make our earth an infinitesimal dot in a solar system that is an infinitesimal dot in a galaxy that is an infinitesimal dot in a quadrant of the cosmos that is an infinitesimal dot in a universe that is an infinitesimal dot in a multiverse that is infinite.

Can we continue to doubt that there is "something" behind, or undergirding, or having given birth to, this magnificent multiverse? Would it not be more logical to assume and conclude that some cause exists behind the effects of the physical realm? And would it be so totally senseless to call this First Cause: "God"?

It is interesting to note that science reports evidence of an extraordinary *intelligence* present in all of life at the cellular, and even the sub-molecular, level. Life seems to *know what it's doing,* and to be doing it deliberately, methodically, consistently, and predictably. Even *in*consistency can be predicted! (see Heisenberg's uncertainty principle.)

And then there is the relatively recent understanding of what is known in quantum physics as the *observer effect.* This states that "nothing that is observed is unaffected by the observer."

What this adds up to is that there are three elements in the "system" that we call "life": *intelligence, design,* and *power.* It is difficult to look closely at any aspect of life as we observe it—either at the micro level of the sub-molecular world or the macro level of the cosmos—without conceding that the manifestations of physicality are simply too sophisticatedly complex, too tightly interlocked, intermixed, and interwoven, too marvelously and massively intricate and interactive, to have been the result of random chance.

It seems clear that the presence of life's patterns is neither "accidental" nor "incidental" in the process of life itself, but that the intelligence and power evidenced in the patterns is the force *behind* that process. Indeed, the Source and the Creator *of* it.

Another Misunderstanding about God: *God Exists and is a Superhuman Male Being*

Even as the statement that God exists is agreed upon by the vast majority of human beings, the exact nature and form, essence and quality, constitution and character of this thing called "God" continue to be open to debate.

One teaching about The Divine—perhaps the one most often reflected in the doctrine of many religions—describes God as a superhuman male being, with human characteristics and proclivities (anger, love, being judgmental, etc.), but with wisdom, power, and abilities far beyond human capacity, or even human understanding.

In some ancient spiritual traditions pre-dating organized religions, The Divine was portrayed as a feminine goddess. And while this portrayal has been brought forward and is held as true even today in certain spiritual movements, the rendition of a male Deity outlined in the paragraph above has been by far the most prevalent.

*

Now comes The Great *What If*. . .

What if God is neither male nor female—and not even a human-like Super Being at all?

Would it make a difference? Does it matter? In the overall scheme of things, would it have any significant impact in our planetary experience?

Yes. First, it would pull the underpinning from a story prevalent across the globe—which is the story of *male supremacy.*

It is no coincidence that most major religions are still run by men. It is no coincidence that the world's largest religion and one of the world's fasted growing religions, still did not allow women in their priesthood as of 2014. It is no coincidence that—minor deviations in this regard notwithstanding—men still pretty much rule the corporate and financial world. It is no coincidence that to this day men continue to dominate the global political scene.

It is no coincidence that even in medicine, science, and academia men continue to vastly outnumber women in places of highest influence, impact, and authority. And it is no coincidence that even where women rise to the level of men in some of society's institutions, they are even now paid less than their male counterparts far too often, although doing the same work.

If we thought that God was not a male, our whole idea of power, might, and glory would be more widely considered to be feminine, as well as masculine, traits. Our depictions of God would not be exclusively of a man with flowing white hair and a flowing white beard in a flowing white robe. Imagine an illustrated Bible with a picture of a female Goddess in it. What would *that* tell our children?

And what if we thought that God was not even a person? What if we relinquished the idea of God as a male *or* a female? What if we accepted as truth the idea that God is not a larger version of human beings at all; not a "person" in any sense of the word? Would that change things in our global expression of spirituality, in our day-to-day experience of religion?

It surely would. It would alter the Father/Child interactions of most of the human beings who believe in God. It would profoundly affect our understanding of our true relationship with divinity.

It would shift our whole notion of how to get what we want from God (if, indeed, we would then think that such a thing was even possible), and it would alter our whole idea of what, if anything, God wants or needs, demands or commands, requires or requests. And *that* would change, in one fell swoop, so much human behavior that our species might have a difficult time recognizing itself.

We would become, in short, a different species in terms of not only our deportment, but our objectives and goals, our measures of "success," our ways of "praying" and interacting with God, and our ideas about where and how we fit into the overall scheme of things.

The search would then begin all over again among the largest number of people (as opposed to the tiny minority who have already begun this process) to redefine God and overhaul our entire approach to interactions with divinity.

Perhaps it is because this kind of massive overhaul of such a critical part of our human experience feels so overwhelming that most of us avoid this new search altogether and remain "stuck" in the same old place forever regarding our understanding of Deity.

Whatever the reason, it is questionable if we are doing ourselves any good hanging out with ideas about God that are thousands of years old.

GOD'S MESSAGE TO THE WORLD

God has been telling us from the very beginning, and it is becoming more clear to us every day, that **humanity's Ancient Cultural Story about God being a superhuman male is plainly and simply inaccurate.**

It is okay now to remove this ancient teaching from our current story, and to stop telling this to ourselves and to our children.

God is obviously (or perhaps not so obviously, to some) not a Big Guy in the Sky who sits on a throne and oversees humanity's countless daily doings, approving some and disapproving others; who hears countless prayers, granting some and denying others; who judges countless souls at their death, rewarding some and punishing others.

God is neither a male nor a female with the appearance, the qualities and the proclivities of humans, yet with supernatural characteristics, powers and abilities. Such an idea of God is simplistic in the extreme.

What, then, is God? Some say this is impossible to know. That is not true. God *can* be known, and God can be experienced. God communicates directly with us, as the founders of our religions have shown, and we can communicate directly with God—as every religion that believes in the power of prayer declares.

God can *be known, and God*
can be experienced.

Here, then, is what God has communicated, and continues to communicate, to humanity about divinity: God is an Essential Essence that permeates everything, the Prime Source of unlimited intelligence and the Prime Force of unlimited creation.

God is at once both The Creator and The Created, a Pure Energy that impacts upon Itself. It is First Cause. It is Every Effect. It is the seat of all wisdom, the wellspring of all desire, the fountainhead of all power, and the origin of all reality.

It is, in a single word, Love.

Its wisdom is activated, Its desire is fulfilled, Its power is evinced, and Its reality is fully, grandly, and gloriously made manifest through the *experience* and the *expression* of Love.

Does this Essential Essence we call "God" have a personality?

Yes.

✳

God's greatness and God's magnificence is God's formlessness. This does not mean, however, that God is not a "personality" to whom we may pray and with whom we may interact. It means, in fact, exactly the opposite.

It is God's essential formlessness that allows God to assume any shape and any form in any moment that it serves the ends of Love for God to assume.

Thus, God can take on the energy of a father's figure, a mother's comfort, a friend's loyalty, a confessor's compassion, a peacemaker's courage, a survivor's strength, a teacher's patience, a compatriot's camaraderie, a lover's intimacy, and a beloved's constancy.

So we see that the fact that God is not, at Its basis, a bigger-than-life human being does not mean that we no longer have anyone to pray to, or to intercede with, or to form a personal relationship with. Quite to the contrary. God can be all things to all people, and if we want a personal God we can pray to, a parent-like God we can ask advice of, or a powerful God we can intercede with, God can and will fill all of those roles for us.

God is all things to all people because God *is* all things *in* all people.

God is *life itself*, which is the expression of Love in physical form. Every expression of *life* is an expression of *Love*. It may not appear that way through the eyes of limited perception, but it is surely, profoundly, and eternally true. (We will look more closely at why and how this can be true in Chapter 25.)

Another Misunderstanding about God: *God Demands Obedience*

LET US EXPLORE NOW THE personal *character* of this Pure Energy called God, this Essential Essence that can form itself into any shape and take on any personality, this Source of Supreme Intelligence and Absolute Power.

As we've noted, the vast majority of the world's people believe that God exists. The question is: What kind of a God is this?

Much of the world believes in a God who is a male super-being *who demands obedience.*

We also note that the vast majority of those who believe in God believe that God is judging, condemning, and punishing when God's demands are not met.

Now comes The Great *What If* . . .

What if God demands nothing,
judges nothing, and punishes nothing?

Would it make a difference? Does it matter? In the overall scheme of things, would it have any significant impact in our planetary experience?

Yes. More violence, more brutality, more killing, and more outright war has been committed in the name of God than under any other banner. If the entire world believed that God demands nothing, judges nothings, and punishes nothing, the spiritual basis for much of the righteousness that underlies, justifies, and motivates humanity's most egregious and self-damaging behaviors would evaporate.

Further, if judgment and punishment were now said to be not part of God's Kingdom, the foundation of humanity's entire legal system would be shaken to the core, with many of the laws in many of our countries having to be rewritten or repealed.

As well, if we embraced the notion that God demands and commands nothing, many of our cultural norms, customs, and prohibitions would be stripped of their moral authority, and would likewise eventually have to be abandoned for lack of any premise or basis.

Nowhere is this better illustrated than in the case of same-gender marriage. Even as restrictions against marriages outside of a person's faith or race were one day held as being "against God's Law"—but are now seen as perfectly acceptable expressions of love (except in some Muslim sects and other ultra-fundamentalist religious communities; recall Chapter 6)—so, too, will gay marriage one day become widely embraced as entirely appropriate between people who deeply love each other. This will occur when the entirety of humanity abandons all notions that an expression of true love that strays from past societal norms somehow breaks God's commandments.

If there *are* no commandments from God, then we can no longer kill, no longer punish, no longer judge, oppress, harm, restrict, limit, or damage others in the name of the Lord. This would wipe out an entire mountain of vindication for a huge catalogue of human cruelties and atrocities.

The question is, would it also remove from humanity's experience a moral compass upon which our species has depended? What would our new moral compass be?

GOD'S MESSAGE TO THE WORLD

God has been telling us from the very beginning, and it is becoming more clear to us every day, that **humanity's Ancient Cultural Story about a God who is demanding and commanding is plainly and simply inaccurate.**

It is okay now to remove this ancient teaching from our current story, and to stop telling this to ourselves and to our children.

God demands and commands nothing. This is because God has no *reason* to demand or command anything. And *this* is because God needs nothing.

God "needs" no experience—emotional, physical, or spiritual—since God is the *source* of every experience God could have. How can the source of something need that thing? How can the Source of Everything need anything? And if the Source of Everything needs nothing, why would It command anything?

It is not as if some behavior of ours, such as obeying God, could cause God to have an experience that God could not have without us exhibiting that behavior. To put this another way, God is not dependent *upon us* for God's nonexistent needs to be met.

There is no reason, then, to believe in a God who is so *dis*pleased in the absence of a particular behavior that we will be punished horribly and eternally.

God is Love, and this love knows neither condition nor limitation. It is not based on receiving anything back, and it is not withheld because God is angry to the point of everlasting condemnation, for the simple reason that God is *never* angry to the point of everlasting condemnation (or ever angry at all).

There are those who say that God demands or commands things not because God needs something, but because *we* need something. Specifically, we need instructions, directions, requirements, and commandments in order to stop ourselves from running amok, and to help us make our lives work.

This viewpoint holds that without commandments and directions, we wouldn't know how to behave—or be willing or *able* to behave in ways that serve our continued survival—because of our very nature.

It is said by some that it is "human nature" to behave irresponsibly and uncontrollably, selfishly and even violently, and that it is only God's requirements and restrictions—and the threat of God's punishment if we don't heed them—that keeps us from being totally self-centered, self-serving, and self-destructive.

Following suit, punishment has become the rationale for all civil laws and government regulations restricting and governing the behavior of people, from stoplights and speed limits that must be obeyed, to product labeling rules that must be followed, to sanitary standards that must be maintained, to workplace regulations that must be followed.

Without these and other behavioral rules being imposed, the conventional wisdom goes, everybody would do as they pleased, no one would be protected, and people everywhere would be the victim of those who are careless or unscrupulous.

Yet are humans incapable of being self-regulating?

The answer is no.

All humans have the innate ability to govern their own behaviors and to adjust them to the degree that they harm no one, while producing maximum positive results for each individual and maximum benefit for the collective. All we have to do is determine to *use* that innate ability. Ironically, what ignites the desire to do so is the *absence* of rules and regulations . . . from God or anyone else.

God understands this. That is why the ultimate gift God has given humanity is free will. *Freedom* is the fundamental nature of divinity. And God knows that humanity will always act in humanity's best interests, once those best interests are made clear.

If you want a wonderful example of this, watch people as they whiz around the traffic circle at the *Arc de Triomphe* in Paris—where there are no lane markings, no traffic lights, no signs showing who goes first or where, and no police officer to direct the endless and rapid flow of vehicles.

Thousands of people make their way around that monument every day in a hectic mish-mash of interweaving iron on tires—and they do not have to be forced by any law or regulation to yield the right-of-way, stop before smashing into others, or go when others have stopped. They do so automatically.

When you know what it is you're trying to do, the preferable and beneficial action to take becomes instantly obvious and very clear to you. That's why there are fewer traffic accidents on that circle than there are on the Champs-Élysées a hundred yards away, where traffic lights abound, lanes are clearly marked, and the way to proceed is guided by rules and regulations.

☀

Humanity on a global scale cannot become clear about its own best interests until humanity on a global scale is clear about what it is trying to do. And this is where we have fallen short. We have not moved to total clarity and mutual agreement on what it is we are "up to" here during our time upon the earth. Once we do, our behaviors will self-modify and self-regulate in ways that will produce maximum effectiveness.

A species that is highly evolved is one that has reached a collective understanding about what is in its highest and best interest, based on a mutually held awareness of what it is seeking to achieve and to experience.

Because we are not at that stage in the development and evolution of humanity, the pressing question today becomes: What could get us there?

The answer is: A letting go of our Ancient Cultural Story about who we are and why we are alive; about the purpose and process of life; about the nature and desire of God.

God told us in *The New Revelations* that in order to get to *that* place, we will need to have the courage to take five huge steps:

Step 1:
Acknowledge that some
of our old beliefs about God
and about life are no longer working.

Step 2:
Acknowledge that there is
something we do not understand
about God and about Life,
the understanding of which
will change everything.

Step 3:
Be willing for a new
understanding of God and Life
to now be brought forth,
an understanding that could produce
a new way of life on this planet.

Step 4:
Be courageous enough to explore
and examine this new understanding,
and, if it aligns with our inner truth
and knowing, to enlarge our belief
system to include it.

Step 5:
Choose to live our lives as a
demonstration of our highest
and grandest beliefs, rather
than as a denial of them.

A *huge* shift in humanity's thinking—perhaps the biggest invitation ever issued *by* life *to* life—would be the accepting, embracing, and adopting of the following spiritually revolutionary statement:

Nothing can occur in all the Universe
that violates the Will of God.

Everything in human theology, virtually every tenet of every religion on the face of the earth, is rooted and built on exactly the opposite thought. God's will *can* be violated, our religions say. This is the foundation of every religious doctrine of judgment, condemnation, and punishment.

Yet the violation of God's will is utterly impossible unless there is something more powerful than God in the universe—something that can *override* God's will. But nothing of the sort exists, for God is the All In All, the Alpha and the Omega, the Beginning and the End, the Sum Total of Everything.

If, therefore, something is happening, it is happening because God has not stopped it from happening. And if God has not stopped something from happening, how can it be said that it is happening against God's will?

Those who say that God *allows* God's will to be thwarted, and that, therefore, it is possible for people to violate the will of God, have rendered themselves blind to a simple logic: If God *allows* something, then it is not against God's will.

You could not lift your little finger if God did not want you to. Everything that happens, therefore, happens because God allows it to, or it wouldn't and *couldn't* be happening.

The theological question thus becomes not whether God allows—and therefore wills—what is happening to be happening, *but why God would allow it.*

The answer is that God's greatest desire is for that fundamental aspect of divinity that we just spoke of—freedom—to be expressed in every moment by every manifestation of divinity. And since God cannot be hurt or damaged in any way by anything at all, God has no reason to place restrictions on the freedom of any of God's creations or creatures.

God also has no reason to judge, condemn, and punish anyone who *uses* that freedom. Indeed, to do so would be to change the definition of freedom itself, so that it would then mean: "The ability to do as you are told, or suffer the consequences."

Yet this is not what freedom means. That is not *freedom* at all.

Freedom is Love demonstrated; it is Love in action. Restriction of any kind is not Love in action, because restriction is limitation, and Love knows no such thing.

Total Love and Absolute Freedom are synonymous, and produce the theological concept known as free will.

God has given all of God's creatures this gift so that God could give Itself the gift of totally experiencing the wonder and the glory of what It Is. Yet free will is obviously *not* free will if the use of it in a particular way produces indescribable and everlasting torture in the fires of hell. Such a response to the use of God's greatest gift to humanity would make a mockery of both the gift and The Giver.

As well, free will means nothing in an environment in which there are no *choices.* If God is to experience Its full wonder and glory, that which is not considered fully wondrous or glorious in human terms must exist alongside of that which is, so to produce a *context* within which wonder and glory itself may be not simply known, but expressed and experienced. Thus, the physical universe has been created as a Contextual Field within which choices become possible.

Another way of saying this is that the Contextual Field that is our universe exists in the way that it does because in the absence of That Which Is Not, That Which Is *is not.*

That is, *it cannot be experienced.*

In the absence of Darkness, Light cannot be experienced. In the absence of Small, Big cannot be experienced. In the absence of There, Here cannot be experienced. In the absence of Slow, Fast cannot be experienced. Nothing can be experienced in the absence of a contrasting element. It can be known theoretically, but it cannot be expressed experientially.

Therefore has God created a universe in which divinity has what *appear* to be exact opposites, or dualities, but are not.

Using an example from our physical reality, we often label things as either "hot" or "cold." These appear to be opposite ends of a polarity, but they are not. They are *degrees* of the *same thing*—called temperature. There is no "duality" in temperature, there is only One Thing, variously expressed.

In much the same way, all manifestations of life are expressions demonstrating degrees, or variations, of the single thing called divinity.

And thus has God invited divinity's human individuations to judge not, and neither condemn, that which seems to oppose them, but to see it as simply another aspect of the Self, providing an opportunity to be a light unto the darkness, that they might know Who They Really Are—and that all those whose lives they touch might know who they really are as well, by the light of this example.

One's free will choosing of any thought, word, or deed need not be, therefore, a demonstration of one's obedience, but may be an acceptance of one's invitation from God to step into the highest demonstration of one's best idea about oneself. With this understanding, what may have been considered one's *burden* may become one's *joy*.

Life becomes an experience of exaltation when one realizes, finally and at last, that neither fear nor obedience are required by God.

Another Misunderstanding about God: *God sees us as imperfect, and we may not return to God in an imperfect state*

MUCH OF THE WORLD believes in a God who is a male super-being who demands obedience, and *who sees us as imperfect because we have not been obedient.*

There are those who go so far as to say that we were *born* imperfect because the *first* humans did not obey God.

Of the world's three largest religions, two—Christianity and Judaism—have taught their followers across the centuries various doctrines declaring that all human souls are subject to death as a punishment for the "ancestral," "inherited," or "original" sin of the first humans.

Modern Judaism (as opposed to Jewish teachers in Talmudic times) rarely teaches of original sin any more, but much of modern Christianity does to this day.

As well, both Christianity and Judaism teach that human beings are now imperfect, regardless of whether they were born that way. Modern Jewish teaching stresses that this is because humans choose to sin later in life, not because they are born in sin, while much Christian teaching still holds that imperfection is the state of our soul upon entry into this world, and this inborn state is what creates an ongoing tendency in humans to sin throughout their lives.

Part of this idea is the notion, supported by some, known as *traducianism*, which declares that God created only one original soul—Adam (Eve was said to have been formed by God from Adam's rib)—and that all other souls derive their basic qualities and tendencies from their parents, and the ancestors before them, through a process by which the qualities of the soul are passed down from one soul to the next, generation to generation.

How did the imperfection that some say is "inherited" originally arise? There are varying versions of the story, but, loosely, it is this:

The first humans, Adam and Eve, were given total freedom, with all of their earthly needs met, in the Garden of Eden. God asked only one thing of them: Do not eat of the fruit of the Tree of Knowledge of Good and Evil. They did. Eve picked an apple and shared it with Adam. The rest, as they say, is history.

The two were driven out of paradise by an angry God, who is said to have cursed their children, their children's children, and their children's children's children—yea, even unto the end of time. God cursed their entire progeny, it was said, with inherited imperfection and physical death—neither of which conditions were aspects of Adam and Eve's reality in paradise.

Thus, imperfection and death became part of the very nature of being human.

Now comes The Great *What If*...

What if God never cursed anyone?
What if no one is born in sin? And what if
God has never seen, and does not now see,
any human being as imperfect in any way?

Would it make a difference? Does it matter? In the overall scheme of things, would it have any significant impact in our planetary experience?

Yes. Of course it would. The first thing it would do is relieve people of any anxiety they may hold about death and about what, if anything, "bad" could happen to them after they leave their body.

Actually, humans wouldn't have any worries about this at all if they had not been told of God's requirement that only perfection is allowed in heaven. But most religions have made it very clear that this requirement is in place, and that there is no getting around it.

The Bible, for instance, tells us directly and unequivocally that God's standard for allowing us to join God in heaven is perfection. The Bible also tells us, at Romans 3:23, that *no human being can meet that standard.* It says that "all have sinned and fall short of the glory of God."

Yet even if we haven't committed one sin in our entire life, there's that bugaboo, *traducianism.* We've got our *inherited* imperfection to deal with.

And as we noted earlier, our beliefs tell us that God has no leeway here. The Law is the Law. The 23rd Psalm says, "Surely goodness and mercy shall follow me all the days of my life," but that does not, presumably, apply after death. Then, mercy apparently has no place. God has no choice but to deny every imperfect soul immediate access to heaven—and since no soul exists in a state of perfection, that means, according to some doctrines, that all souls are initially denied access.

This doesn't mean they *never* get into heaven, however. We earlier described a place called Purgatory, where souls are said to be sent prior to entering heaven in order to be purified by having the blemish of their sins eradicated through a process of suffering in payment for them.

It should be made clear here that not all of the world's religions teach of the need for the soul to suffer in order to compensate for offenses. Many teach of a God who admits us into heaven at once if we sincerely repent of our sins. But if we don't . . . .

So the overall pronouncement is this: We are imperfect beings. We should stand before the throne of God in trembling and in shame, with the hope that our imperfections and transgressions will be forgiven. If we do not do what is necessary to purify our souls and return them to perfection, now or in the hereafter (such as by submitting to abject suffering in payment for our sins in Purgatory), we're not getting back Home. It's as simple as that.

Now if the huge number of people (we are talking billions here) who believe this is true altered their belief, fear, shame, and guilt would be lifted from the hearts of both innocent children and sad adults who carry as a burden their identity as being undeserving of reuniting with God in heaven.

And if the third question in the "what if" above were to be embraced as humanity's reality, the lack of self-worth that now sponsors so much of our species' dysfunctional, self-defeating, and hurtful behaviors would at last be healed. It is clear that this would cause the largest number of those behaviors to disappear.

GOD'S MESSAGE TO THE WORLD

God has been telling us from the very beginning, and it is becoming more clear to us every day, that **humanity's Ancient Cultural Story about God seeing us as imperfect, and therefore not allowing us back into heaven unless and until we have been purified, is plainly and simply inaccurate.**

It is okay now to remove this ancient teaching from our current story, and to stop telling this to ourselves and to our children.

We are not born in sin, nor do we inherit sinful tendencies through a lineage of souls going back to a purported First Misbehaver. "Ancestral guilt" is a figment of our religious imagination. The story of Adam and Eve is a fiction as well.

God did not throw anyone out of paradise, and one look at the world around you will show you that human beings are still living in a paradise. They are despoiling it step-by-step, to be sure, but even with all of that, nothing compares to a sunrise or a sunset, to an eagle's glide or a butterfly's flutter, to the fragrance of a rose or the smell of the morning dew. There is nothing more stunning than the quiet beauty of an unexpected snowfall, or the noisy beauty of expected waves pounding upon a sandy shore. We watch both with awe, as well we should, for we are clear we are seeing something exceeding magnificence.

And that is just the beginning, just the top of a long list of treasures that this paradise called the earth will always hold, if we will but hold them *as* treasures, keeping them safe from disassembling and destruction.

The beauty of this world is enhanced beyond measure by the beauty of you. *Nothing* is imperfect about you. Nothing you have ever thought, nothing you have ever said, nothing you have ever done. It is all perfect, because it is all part of the process of your personal evolution—and, on a larger scale, of the evolution of the human species.

Even as all the "failed" experiments of all the scientists in all the laboratories across the globe are perfect, in that they are steps in the producing of an ultimately important and highly beneficial result . . . even as the mathematical miscalculations and spelling errors of all the children in all the schools of the world are perfect, in that they are steps in the producing of the highest scores . . . so, too are the "mistakes" of humanity as a whole seen as perfect in the eyes of God—steps in the evolutionary process of *all life everywhere.*

All that was ever thought or said or done by any and every human being—even the worst of it—has been the product of the innocence of a species so young, its members did not know any better; they did not understand how to get that for which they yearned, they did not comprehend how to escape or evade that which they wished to avoid.

This is difficult for many people to accept. The idea that fully grown humans have done these things, that some of us have acted in these ways, because of extreme immaturity, is challenging to our belief that surely, grown men and women know right from wrong, and don't have to be told that killing others and destroying everything in their path is not the way to achieve their goals, what*ever* they may be.

We assert that people should know better because we like to think of humans as highly evolved. In fact, humanity has just emerged from its infancy.

In their book *New World New Mind,* Robert Ornstein and Paul Ehrlich placed this in perspective in one mind-boggling paragraph:

> Suppose Earth's history were charted on a single year's calendar, with midnight January 1

> representing the origin of Earth and midnight December 31 the present. Then each day of Earth's "year" would represent 12 million years of actual history. On that scale, the first form of life, a simple bacterium, would arise sometime in February. More complex life-forms, however, come much later; the first fishes appear around November 20. The dinosaurs arrive around December 10 and disappear on Christmas Day. The first of our ancestors recognizable as human would not show up until the *afternoon of December 31.* Homo sapiens—our species—would emerge at around 11:45 p.m. . . . and *all that has happened in recorded history* would occur in *the final minute of the year.*

As you can see, we are an astonishingly young species, and, not surprisingly, very immature.

And so, we have used violence to produce outcomes that we were sure justified its use (even if it meant death to millions of innocent men, women, and children).

And so, we have used domination—sometimes cruel, heartless domination—to generate results we were sure were desirable to experience (even if it subjected the entire population of a country or an area to ruthless suppression, persecution, and maltreatment).

And so, we have used self-interest—sometimes unmitigated, unbridled self-interest—to generate a level of sufficiency for ourselves that we were sure we deserved (even if millions of others had to go without, given the global economic model that we have empowered).

And so, we have used self-righteousness—sometimes appalling, execrable self-righteousness—to generate a sense of self-worth that we were sure we deserved (even as we told others that they were unworthy and were going to be condemned by God to hell).

⁂

These childish, almost infantile, behaviors are seen by God as the uncontrolled and irrational tantrums of an unenlightened species, a breed of sentient beings in the primitive, primeval, primordial stages of its maturational process.

Put simply, The Divine perfectly well understands the nature of what it is to be human. Even as we understand how a three-year-old could knock over the milk reaching anxiously for the chocolate cake because it wants the cake so badly, so does God understand completely how we could act as some of us have acted, reaching for what we have wanted so badly.

Even the wanting of some things, in and of itself, could be considered "wrong" by judgmental humans, just as a child's wanting more cake than his little sister might be considered "wrong." In our human value system, he shouldn't want more than everyone else. And he certainly would be considered "wrong" for trying to get it by bullying his way to it. Yet the wise parent understands the not-yet-mature desire of the older brother, and does not send him to his room for the remainder of his childhood.

God sees us just as we see our children: in the process of maturing, but nonetheless whole, complete, and perfect just as we are right now. There is nothing we have to be, nothing we have to say, and nothing we have to do to gain the love of our Creator, who adores us even as we misbehave. There are no credentials we must acquire in order to be qualified to return to heaven. Our credential is our *existence.* Nothing more is needed.

That message is important enough to be repeated.

There are no credentials
we must acquire in order
to be qualified to return to heaven.
Our credential is our existence.
Nothing more is needed.

⁂

Again, this is hard to believe and difficult to accept by a race of beings conditioned to imagine that perfect justice requires condemnation and punishment—including, in some cases, death.

You must remember that human beings are of such infantile comprehension that they will claim that the killing of people by the state is the way to teach people that killing people is bad.

You must remember that human beings are of such infantile comprehension that they will claim that the use of weapons of mass destruction in a preemptive strike by one country is the way to teach another country that to have weapons of mass destruction is bad.

You must remember that human beings are of such infantile comprehension that they will claim that strict adherence to a religion that teaches intolerance of any other religion is the way to teach the world that intolerance is bad.

⁂

A God of Unconditional Love is utterly incomprehensible to a species that has still not learned to love itself enough to stop destroying itself.

We cannot believe that God would forgive us for that which we cannot forgive each other.

It is nonetheless true that even if we have done what we, or others, consider to be truly horrible things during our time on the earth . . . even then, God will welcome us back Home.

There are a number of very good reasons that this will be true, and we'll be examining them in the chapters just ahead as we continue to explore humanity's misunderstandings about God. For now, please read this, given to us by Jesus.

I know that you are probably very familiar with this tale, but please read it anyway.

> A certain man had two sons. And the younger of them said to his father, "Father, give me the portion of goods that falls to me." So he divided among both of his sons their inheritance.
>
> Not many days after, the younger son gathered all his things together, journeyed to a far country, and there wasted his possessions with prodigal living. But when he had spent all, there arose a severe famine in that land, and he began to be in want.
>
> Then he went and found work with a citizen of that country, and the man sent him into the fields to feed swine. And he would gladly have filled his stomach with the pods that the swine ate, but no one gave him anything.
>
> Then he came to himself, thinking: "How many of my father's hired servants have bread enough and to spare, and I perish with hunger! I will arise and go to my father, and will say to him, 'Father, I have

sinned against heaven and before you, and I am no longer worthy to be called your son. Make me like one of your hired servants."

And he arose and went to his father. But when he was still a great way off, his father saw him and had compassion, and ran and fell on his neck and kissed him. And the son said to him, "Father, I have sinned against heaven and in your sight, and am no longer worthy to be called your son."

But the father said to his servants, "Bring out the best robe and put it on him, and put a ring on his hand and sandals on his feet. And bring the fatted calf here and kill it, and let us eat and be merry; for this son of mine was dead and is alive again; he was lost and is found." And they began to be merry.

Now the father's older son was in the field, working. And as he came and drew near to the house, he heard music and dancing. So he called one of the servants and asked what these things meant.

And the servant said to him, "Your brother has come home, and because he was safe and sound, your father has killed the fatted calf."

But the second son was angry and would not go in. Therefore his father came out and pleaded with him. So the second son answered and said to his father, "Lo, these many years I have been serving you; I never transgressed your commandment at any time; and yet you never gave me even a young goat, that I might make merry with my friends. But as soon as this son of yours came, who has devoured your livelihood with harlots, you killed the fatted calf for him."

And his father said to him, "Son, you are always with me, and all that I have is yours. It was right

> that we should make merry and be glad, for your brother was dead and is alive again, and was lost and is found."

To me, this is the single most important story in the Bible. It says everything important that Jesus wanted us to know about God. But Jesus knew that people rarely understood, much less embraced, really deep truths if heard only once. So he made his same point again and again, saying things like . . .

> What man among you, having an hundred sheep, if he lose one of them, doth not leave the ninety and nine in the wilderness, and go after that which is lost, until he find it?
>
> And when he cometh home, he calleth together *his* friends and neighbors, saying unto them, "Rejoice with me; for I have found my sheep which was lost!"

Does this include the worst of us? The "black sheep" of our human family?

Yes.

And so, we can rest easy. We will not be abandoned because we became lost, and we will not be rejected when we finally return Home, no matter what we may have done while we were away.

In Chapter 22, I have a big surprise for you. It will clarify all of this in thirteen words. But don't jump ahead. The chapters between here and there will place those stunning thirteen words into context. They're going to mean much more to you if you "read your way" to them rather than "jump" to them.

☀

Parables and stories are one way of getting an idea across. Poetry is another. It bypasses the mind and seeps right into the heart. I have placed the following poem in other books of mine, and I am placing it in this book again, because—like the parable above—a message wondrously crafted cannot be heard too often.

I am blessed to be married to the American poet, Em Claire. This is her offering:

LONG AT SEA

I left Home so long ago now
that I would not recognize my own face.
I constructed the Boat of my Life
and I set out
into the open sea,
waving to all who knew
that the seas would give me
everything I could handle,
and everything I could not—
and yet they waved, and I set out
into the open sea
in the Boat of My Life:
built from Soul, crafted by Heart.
And with great innocence I pushed off
into the open sea
and have been away from my Home
so long now that I would not recognize my own face—
but I know that Home,
Home
remembers me.

(From the book and CD *Home Remembers Me*,
available at *www.EmClairePoet.com*)

Another Misunderstanding about God: *God requires us to believe in God, and to worship God in a specific way*

MUCH OF THE WORLD believes in a God who is a male superbeing who demands obedience, who says we are imperfect because we have *not* been obedient, and who tells us that in order for us to be in God's good graces (and thus, eligible for admission into heaven), *we must meet certain requirements.*

Among those requirements are that we believe in God in a certain way, and worship God in a particular fashion.

What this comes down to is that we must belong to a specific religion—or at least, hold true to its tenets.

The thought that we even *need* to be in a good place with God arises out of the idea we explored above: that only absolute purity and total perfection is allowable or present in heaven, and that this probably does not describe us—so we'd better do something about it.

This thought, in turn, emerges from the other thought explored earlier: that we entered this world in a *state* of impurity, branded at birth with Original Sin, Inherited Imperfection, or Ancestral Guilt, and that we all have in any event offended God with our own sins during our own lives.

And *this* thought surfaces from a deeply-held belief that we *can* sin, and that God *can* be offended.

From these congealed notions is born a deep concern in the hearts of many people that we are *not* in God's good graces now. And so we look, individually and as a collective, for ways in which we can *get* into God's good graces—before it is too late.

The popularity of religions is based on this yearning, and on their promises that they can produce this result.

Religions, we are told, are our passports into heaven. All we have to do is follow their mandates, live according to their guidelines, obey their rules, and respond affirmatively to their injunctions.

Dramatically increasing the stakes in all this is the statement of some denominations that their religion offers the *only* way to achieve what is called "salvation."

We are told that if we do not believe what *they* teach, if we do not embrace *their* doctrine, if we do not accept *their* canon, creed, and credo as the truth, the whole truth, and nothing but the truth, we are condemned by God to everlasting damnation.

There is no question about this among the faithful within those denominations: We *must* believe in God and worship God in a certain and particular way or our eternal soul is eternally doomed.

⁂

Now comes The Great *What If* . . .

What if God does not need to be worshipped,
and does not need to have humans believe

in God in any certain way? What if God does not need human beings to believe in God at all?

Would it make a difference? Does it matter? In the overall scheme of things, would it have any significant impact in our planetary experience?

Yes, of course it would. If we let go of the thought that one way is the only way to worship God and get to heaven, the spiritual self-righteousness that appears deeply embedded in humanity's experience of God would virtually disappear. And absent that self-righteousness, all of the religious wars and inter-denominational struggles, the ruthless and senseless killing that has soiled the pages of human history for millennia, would likewise ultimately disappear.

If we felt that we didn't even need to *believe* in God for God to welcome us back Home, we could then enter into whatever belief in God we might develop—if, indeed, we chose to embrace such a belief at all—and do so as an expression of pure joy and absolute wonderment, rather than an outgrowth of angst or a product of trepidation. A loss of fear about what will happen if we do not profess a belief in God would spell the end of all fear-based religions.

Indeed, as the love-me-or-else threat was taken out of our experience of God, our entire relationship with The Divine would shift dramatically, putting us into a genuine friendship with God in which our worried trembling would be replaced by our empowerment.

On another level, if we held the thought that God has no need for our worship, our species would stop seeing the whole notion of "worship" as a good thing, but would view it, accurately, as the kind of subjugating human activity that denies our own divinely bestowed magnificence—to say nothing of our own *presence* in that which we say we adore.

This elevating of the human self to its rightful place of awesome *inclusion* in the expression that is God would reshape humanity's basic identity, altering our species' understanding and expression of *itself.* And it would do this so completely as to remove and eliminate selfish, hurtful, malicious, or malevolent behavior from the human experience forever. We would suddenly know who we really are, and who everyone else is, and we would treat ourselves and everyone else much differently.

This is, in fact, what has occurred within the civilizations of all highly evolved beings in the universe. The effect that such a shift in beliefs would have on the planet would be to, at last, *civilize* civilization.

GOD'S MESSAGE TO THE WORLD

God has been telling us from the very beginning, and it is becoming more clear to us every day, that **humanity's Ancient Cultural Story about God demanding that we worship, believe in, and approach God in a certain and particular way is plainly and simply inaccurate.**

It is okay now to remove this ancient teaching from our current story, and to stop telling this to ourselves and to our children.

God does not care what religion we belong to (or whether we belong to any religion at all). Religions are the inventions and conventions of humanity.

God doesn't care what we believe about God (or whether we believe in God at all). Beliefs are the inventions and conventions of humanity.

God doesn't look to us to provide God with something that God needs (because God needs nothing at all). Needs are the inventions and conventions of humanity.

The need to be worshipped (to say nothing of the *command* to be loved) could only be the characteristic of an insecure, unfulfilled, imperious, tyrannical ruler—which cannot possibly describe the God of this universe.

The need to be approached in a single and specific way, making every other approach (no matter how sincere the motive, no matter how pure the intent, no matter how arduous the effort) not only insufficient, but a cause for *judgment, condemnation* , and *damnation,* could only be the characteristic of a totally unreasonable, utterly intolerant, preposterously hypersensitive, unbelievably small-minded, and insanely draconian despot—which cannot possibly describe the God of this universe.

The idea that God *demands* to be loved defies all reason and logic. Yet it is held by many, for it is written, in what has been labeled as *The Greatest Commandment*: "Thou shalt love the Lord thy God with all thine heart, and with all thy soul, and with all thy might."

So let it be said clearly and without equivocation: The God of this universe—by *virtue* of *being* God—needs or requires the adulation of no one. As well, the God of this universe—by *virtue* of *being* God—has nothing to lose by welcoming any soul who arrives at divinity by any path, and is nothing but overjoyed when any soul has found its way back Home by realizing, accepting, and assuming its true identity.

The idea that God rejects everyone except those who come to God by one singular and particular path is simply mistaken. It defies all rational thought and directly contradicts the definition of Love.

The idea that God rejects everyone except those who come to God by one singular and particular path is simply mistaken.

The good news is that our Deity is not the God of the brand name.

God's love, God's acceptance, and God's joy in us is not dependent upon what words we say in prayer, what name we invoke in supplication, or what faith we embrace in hopefulness.

In the eyes of God a Jew is as good as a Christian, a Christian is as good as a Muslim, a Muslim is as good as a Buddhist, a Buddhist is as good as a Mormon, a Mormon is as good as a Bahá'í, and an atheist is as good as all of the above.

That Which Is is That Which Is, and neither its Isness, nor its joy and bliss *in being* the Isness, is dependent upon any particular expression in any particular way of any particular part of the Isness.

☼

Let us go even further. It is not even necessary for human beings to have *any* belief that there *is* a God in order for God's blessings to flow. The flowing of God's blessings is God's greatest joy, and it is a process that is uninterrupted and eternal.

It has nothing whatsoever to do with our love for God, and everything to do with God's love for us.

Again, this may be the toughest concept for human beings to accept. The largest number of us just can't seem to embrace the notion that divine love flows freely to all, without exception, requirement, or condition of any kind.

Or, in a remarkable inversion, many declare that God's love *does* flow freely to all, and that God's condemnation and punishment of His subjects for not believing in God, or for any wrongdoing, is a *demonstration* of His love.

It is only through such convoluted theological architecture that the idea of a God kind and good can be constructed and preserved—although is it questionable if such preservation has been achieved at the level that those who have constructed this theology might have wished. It seems far more evidentiary that the idea of a God kind and good has been simply forfeited by religion, and that this is the chief reason for the rejection, by millions, of the idea of any sort of God at all.

This is one of the greatest sorrows to have befallen the human race, for it has robbed so many members of the species of their greatest resource, therefore crippling the species itself immeasurably.

We shall explore this effect next.

Another Misunderstanding about God: *God is vengeful and God's love can turn to wrath*

THIS IS AN EXTENSION of an earlier belief. Much of the world believes in a God who is a male super-being, who demands obedience, who says we are imperfect because we have *not* been obedient, and who tells us that in order for us to be in God's good graces (and thus, eligible for admission into heaven), we must meet certain very specific requirements—*and whose love turns to wrath if those requirements are not met.*

A search of many of the holy books of the human species produces countless references to "the wrath of God" in many of the world's religious traditions.

In the Jewish tradition we are told at Nahum 1:2 that "Adonai is a jealous and vengeful God. Adonai avenges; he knows how to be angry. Adonai takes vengeance on his foes and stores up wrath for his enemies."

In the Christian tradition we are told in John 3:35-36 that, "He that believeth on the Son hath everlasting life: and he that believeth not the Son shall not see life; but the wrath of God abideth on him."

In the Islamic traditions we are told at Verse 005:060 about: ". . . those whom Allah has cursed, those upon whom fell the wrath of Allah, those whom Allah turned into monkeys and pigs, and the devotees of the arrogant and the evil. Their plight is the worst; they are the farthest away from the straight path."

In the Mormon tradition we are told in Mosiah 3:36 of those who "have drunk out of the cup of the wrath of God, which justice could no more deny unto them than it could deny that Adam should fall because of his partaking of the forbidden fruit; therefore, mercy could have claim on them no more forever."

Things are considered pretty serious when scriptures that we call holy tell us of a Deity that we call merciless. Small wonder that people throughout history have been nervous about offending God. Even Moses was known to have said in a prayer to God: ". . . we are consumed by thine anger, and by thy wrath are we troubled." (Psalm 90:7)

Indeed, we are. This idea of God's merciless anger permeates human considerations of The Divine, and has done so for centuries.

⁂

Now comes The Great *What If*. . .

What if God has never displayed,
and never will express or
experience, wrath?

Would it make a difference? Does it matter? In the overall scheme of things, would it have any significant impact in our planetary experience?

Yes. Of course it would. It would allow us to believe in a God whose love is unconditional and is never withdrawn for any reason at all—and certainly not for our *beliefs.*

This, in turn, would give human beings, at last, an accurate model of the true nature of love, and a wonderful example of how to love one other. Right now many humans use their understanding of how *God* loves *us* as *their* model of how *they* should love one another.

Accepting the notion that God's love is unconditional would mean that a display of human wrath for any reason could no longer rely for its justification on the teaching that God has brought His wrath to bear on humanity time and time again. (You will recall that the Bible indicates that over two million people were killed at the hand or the command of God.)

At the level of individual life partnerships and romantic relationships, a new way of loving each other would have a *demonstrable basis* if humans were not told over and over again about God's wrath. That new basis would be God's unconditional love. What a model we would finally have! Someone who loves us *no matter what.*

Fear, too, would leave the human heart forever if we thought that the experience of love—whether the love of another human being or the love of God—was forever.

If we thought that God had no wrath, little children could go to bed no longer having to worry about what will happen if they don't live until morning. The prayer, "Now I lay me down to sleep, I pray to God my soul to keep. If I should die before I wake, I pray to God my soul to take . . ." could be changed to: "Now I lay me down to sleep, I know that God my soul will keep. And if I die before I wake, I know that God my soul will take."

If we thought that God expresses no wrath, billions of adults could go to bed no longer feeling the urge to beg Mary, the mother of Jesus, to "pray for us sinners, now and at the hour of our death."

Thus, Supplication Theology would be replaced by Application Theology.

Supplication Theology is a theology in which we are placed in the position of a supplicant, continually asking God, begging God, entreating with God for one thing or another.

Application Theology is a theology in which we *apply* in our lives what we know to be true about our relationship to God: that God lives in us, through us, as us, and that the qualities of divinity are ours to apply in our daily lives, including wisdom, clarity, knowledge, creativity, power, abundance, compassion, patience, understanding, needlessness, peace, and love.

GOD'S MESSAGE TO THE WORLD

God has been telling us from the very beginning, and it is becoming more clear to us every day, that **humanity's Ancient Cultural Story about God's wrath is plainly and simply inaccurate.**

It is okay now to remove this ancient teaching from our current story, and stop telling this to ourselves and to our children.

The fact is that God has no reason to experience or express wrath. When you *are* everything, *have* everything, *created* everything, *experience* everything, and can *express* everything that you wish to express, what can there be to be filled with rage about?

When you *want* nothing, *need* nothing, *require* nothing, *demand* nothing, and *command* nothing, what can there be for you to feel betrayed about?

Finally, when there is nothing else in *existence* except *You*, who is there for you to be rageful *with?* Whom shall you punish? Shall the right hand slap the left?

The idea of a wrathful God rests on a notion that God cares what you do or don't do as one of billions of creatures in one of billions of moments on one of billions of planets in one of billions of sectors of a cosmos that is one billion trillion times the size of your home star. And not only that God cares, but that God cares *so much* as to be *deeply wounded* and *grievously offended* if your behavior does not live up to what is expected—nay, *commanded*—of you.

That would be akin to saying that *you* are concerned with one grain of sand out of all the grains of sand on all the beaches in all the world. You may *love* the sand and *all* its grains because they are part of the wonder and beauty of all the world's beaches, but you certainly wouldn't be filled with wrath if one of those grains was not reflecting the sunlight the way it was designed to. And you certainly wouldn't be furious if you knew that this was but a temporary condition in any event, lasting no more than a nanosecond in the eternal span of that grain of sand's existence.

The idea of a wrathful God not only depends upon our acceptance of the thought that God has a preference in the matter of our behaviors, but also on the notion that all of our behaviors and all of their consequences *have not already taken place.*

A wrathful deity can only be considered within totally artificial constructs of space and time. Yet in the universal

Here/Now, God cannot *become* wrathful based on something that has *just happened*, but would have to *always* be wrathful based on all the things with which God is said to disagree, since everything that has ever happened, is happening now, and ever will happen is occurring simultaneously in the eternal and singular moment of Evernow.

It is true that God is always being *something* in Evernow, but "wrath" is not it. God is Love, eternal and unchanging.

Not wrath. Love.

Love unconditional.

The Essential Essence. The Prime Force. The Pure Energy. The Singular Element. The Only Thing There Is.

To gravitate toward this new and revolutionary holding of the Divine Reality and the Deity experience, one would have to release oneself from the notion that God is a creature of moods, whose temperament depends on what is happening at a particular time on a particular day in a particular life in a particular place on a particular planet in a particular solar system of a particular galaxy within a particular quadrant of a particular universe.

To help you move to this new and revolutionary holding, remember this always:

God is Love,
eternal and unchanging.
Not wrath. Love.
Love unconditional.

There is a third notion we must deal with. It is the stubborn belief that there is something called "divine justice," which can be violated, or that divine perfection can somehow be irrevocably marred, by a single event in the single life of . . . here we go again . . . a single being on a single planet in a single solar system of a single galaxy within a single quadrant of a single universe.

We are told by some religions that it is this violation or marring that God finds intolerable and unacceptable, and which must therefore be rectified and reconciled.

Yet God tells us (as opposed to what religions tell us) that perfection *can't* be marred, because perfection is the natural state of things and the everlasting condition and reality.

In truth, no one thing is better than another, but all things are simply what they are: reflections of a perfectly functioning universe in a perfectly demonstrating manifestation of a perfectly existing reality, one thing leading inexorably to another in a never-ending process called evolution.

How can any and every reality be perfect? Simple. If no one and nothing requires anything or something other than What Is. And this is the natural state of things.

In Ultimate Reality that which is divine requires and desires nothing other than What Is, for the very good reason that What Is is the sum total of all possibilities, all events, all circumstances, all conditions, all experiences, and all expressions of life in any and all forms, all at once.

A rainy day is no less perfect than a sunny day, for it is the rainy day that makes the glory of the sunny day joyful, and the heat of the sunny day that makes the cooling of the rainy day welcome.

It is the mistake on her multiplication tables at age nine that produces the mathematical genius teaching advanced calculus at MIT at age thirty-four.

And yes, it is even the horror of the worst of human experiences that has given birth to the best of our species' expressions as we evolve across the decades, centuries, and millennia.

Across the span of all existence, one circumstance or event produces, eventually, an awareness that authors another circumstance or event, and the master lives life without judgment or condemnation of that process, nor of any person or occurrence that is part of it, but rather, sees the grander mosaic.

"Justice" and "perfection" are human constructions created within the context of relative values. The idea of divine justice depends upon a preceding idea that some things are "right" and some things are "wrong" in the mind of God. Yet such an idea does not exist in the realm of the spiritual, which is also a realm of the Absolute, where everything is experienced Here/Now, and the only energy is Absolute Love.

Every spiritual master knows this, which is why all spiritual masters have said, each in their own way: *Judge not, and neither condemn.* You have already heard this message before here—and you will hear it again before these proceedings are concluded—for it rests at the heart of everything the human race is invited to embrace in its new understanding of God.

The question is, does "judge not, and neither condemn" apply as well to God?

The answer that most religionists have given us is, no. *Humans* are not to judge, but *God* is *expected* to judge.

Yet is this how everything is really supposed to work? And if so, why? How did it get to be this way?

Another Misunderstanding about God: *God was at war with the Devil, and that's how this all began*

Virtually every major religion teaches of a personality or a creature that is not God. This creature has been called by many names, some of them: Satan, Lucifer, Beelzebub, the Devil, the Prince of Darkness, the Evil Spirit, the Fallen Angel, and the Tempter. This creature is said to be in a constant battle with God for the souls of humanity.

To use but one example, the theology of the Christian Congregation of Jehovah's Witnesses teaches that this creature called the Devil existed originally as a perfect angel, but later developed feelings of pride and self-importance, then persuaded the first woman, Eve, and through her, the first man, Adam, to disobey God. It was this decision to rebel against God's sovereignty and obey the Devil instead that made Adam and Eve sinners, causing them to transmit a sinful nature to all of their future offspring.

God could have simply destroyed the Devil then and there, and killed the disobedient couple as well. (He did, after all, kill two million people at His hand or His command, if we are to believe the Bible.) But, according to the theology of Jehovah's Witnesses, God decided to allow time to test the loyalty of the rest of humankind, and to prove to the rest of the universe that man cannot be independent of God successfully, that man is lost without God's laws and standards and can never bring peace to the earth, and that Satan was a deceiver, murderer, and liar.

Why God would need to test anything, much less the loyalty of a just-born species (which would be akin to humans having to test the "loyalty" of a three-day-old baby), is not explained. Nor are we told why God would need to "prove" anything to the rest of the universe—although this aspect of the theology does present us with the interesting assertion that there is intelligent life elsewhere in the universe. Otherwise, why bother?

This science-fictionesque story of God kicking God's own lovingly produced creations out of paradise is not limited to a single denomination's theology, but is widely taught in similar form in the Origination Story of many religions and cultures.

In some Korean homes, to offer a separate example, the story of Mago's Garden is told. This tale speaks of a Deity who created a paradise and then placed in it human creations of different colors, like flowers in a beautiful garden. Because of their differences, however, these creatures fought amongst themselves, and so, in Her disappointment and anger, Mago banished Her creations from paradise, separating them and sending them to different places upon the earth, telling them that they may return to the Garden only when they learn to exist together harmoniously. According to the continuation of this story, the people of a different color upon the earth have been trying to find a way to do so ever since.

Each of our Origination Stories tells of a God who created something that, in the end, turned out to be not so good. Improbable as this sounds, the insistence on this story continues. In some accounts of this tale, what turned bad was an angel named Lucifer; in others it was God's own children; and in still others, it was both. In some stories, God was at war with the Devil, and, being victorious, threw him into hell forever, and it is from this horrible place that he now competes for men's souls.

In any case, humanity's fundamental Origination Story is, as I said, the story of a good plan gone bad—of something that is not divine, but emerged *from* The Divine, that has failed to demonstrate or reflect qualities *of* The Divine, and that now seeks to tempt all of us to do the same.

⁂

Now comes The Great *What If . . .*

What if there is no such thing
as Satan, the Devil, Lucifer, or any
"evil spirit"—and what if that which is
not divine simply does not exist?

Would it make a difference? Does it matter? In the overall scheme of things, would it have any significant impact in our planetary experience?

Yes. Without the existence of a wicked entity or a force for evil that is said to exist in Ultimate Reality, the entire mythology of God's battle with The Darkness would disintegrate, and with it the whole idea of the eternal struggle of good vs. evil.

A news story in August 2014 from the Internet website, TheSpectrum.com, illustrates how deeply this idea has become ingrained in the human culture—and offers us an impeccable example of a point made in the very first chapter of this book. There, I said that it's not a small thing to be wrong about God, because a striking number of the decisions made by billions of people across the globe are made within the context of what they believe about God, and about what God wants. If you think I may have overstated the case, I offer this: "Nevada cattle rancher Cliven Bundy told members of the Independent American Party gathered to hear him Saturday that the April confrontation between his family, federal agencies and Bundy's armed militia supporters was part of an age-old battle between good and evil," the news article on The Spectrum said.

You may recall that Mr. Bundy was ordered by the federal government to cease grazing his cattle on government-owned land. Mr. Bundy refused, and his refusal made the national news, drawing people with loaded guns from far and wide to stand up to the government with him. Or, in Mr. Bundy's own words: "There was people from almost every state in this United States was there. Some of them told me they'd traveled for 40 hours to get there. Why did they come? . . . Because they felt like they needed to. They was spiritually touched."

Mr. Bundy was further quoted in the news story as asking the group he was addressing: "If our (U.S.) Constitution is an inspired document by our Lord Jesus Christ, then isn't it scripture?"

"Yes," a chorus of voices replied. "Isn't it the same as the Book of Mormon and the Bible?" Bundy asked. "Absolutely," the audience answered, according to The Spectrum website.

The armed standoff with federal enforcement officers (who, by the way, backed down) mirrors the same cultural story that starts all our wars.

Human wars are based on—and, in fact, *require*—the characterization of people and positions as "good" and "evil" in order for humans to be sufficiently motivated to violate their own basic nature, which is to *never hurt or damage anyone or anything.*

A "reverence for life" exists at the core of every sentient being, and the only way to get such a being to act against this internal impulse is to convince that being that it is doing "good" by acting in a way that the entity itself would call "evil" if the same actions were taken against it.

Much of humanity's dysfunctional behavior around violence and war has arisen out of humanity's religions having adopted a story of a war in heaven between God and Satan in which God was victorious, resulting in the Fallen Angel being driven out of paradise.

As we have recounted here now several times (following the ongoing example of several religions), the Fallen Angel was not destroyed, however, but, according to the mythology, was allowed to continue to exist as the Prince of Darkness and the Chief of Demons, who *to this day continues to struggle with God* in a battle for human souls.

Fascinatingly, this is characterized as a battle that Satan can *win*. And when he does, the souls who succumb to his temptations are sent to join him in the everlasting fires of hell.

The Bible is replete with statements about hell—which assertions are put forth as vital doctrine (Heb. 6:1, 2), describing hell as a real, literal place of fire and torment (Jude 3, 7; Rev. 14: 1 0; 20:10-15; 21:8); telling us it is where those who knew not Christ would suffer everlasting damnation (2 Thess. 1:8, 9); and warning us that to this day this is a punishment that lasts forever for those who reject Christ (Matt. 13:41, 42; 18:8, 9; 25:41-46; Luke 16:19-31).

And so, religion has been urgently advising us for centuries that we must do all we can to avoid the snares of the Devil.

The idea of intrinsic good vs. inherent evil has thus become a foundational element of the human Cultural Story, as has the notion that God is in a struggle with the Devil, which struggle justifies and allows God's administration of horrible-beyond-description punishment to those who fall prey to Satan's temptations and do not seek forgiveness in a specifically prescribed manner. It is what gives human beings the moral grounds to administer horrible-beyond-description punishment to those whom *they* designate to be *their* enemies.

What's good enough for God, after all, should certainly be good enough for us.

Thus, our species has found a spiritual basis for all manner of human barbarity, and offers God's example as complete vindication of many of its cruelties.

Remove the idea of evil from the constructions and stories of Ultimate Reality and the cornerstone of cruelty crumbles, its rationale lost, its basis dissolved, its justification juxtaposed with an Ultimate Reality where nothing but Love exists, nothing but Love *ever* existed, and nothing but Love ever *will* exist.

The entire script about evil being at war with good, and about an angel who was in a struggle with God in the Kingdom of heaven, is derived from the idea that something which is *not* God can exist.

This idea gives rise to a corollary notion that "sin," understood to be an offense against God, is possible—that it is possible for the Most Powerful Being in the universe (indeed, the

Creator of the universe) to become upset because one being out of seven billion on one of several trillion planets did not go to Mass on Sunday, or failed to travel to Mecca during his lifetime, or fell in love with another being of the same gender.

This construction, in turn, leads to the dubious conclusion that punishment by God will and must ensue as retribution for such offenses, thereby balancing the "scales of justice" and ensuring that in God's Kingdom, everything exists in a state of purity and perfection.

The irony is that a punishment horrible and everlasting is wildly out of proportion to many of humanity's supposed "offenses" (such as coming to God with purity in one's heart, but by the wrong religion). The sad paradox is that this is everything *but* an expression of purity and perfection.

GOD'S MESSAGE TO THE WORLD

God has been telling us from the very beginning, and it is becoming more clear to us every day, that **humanity's Ancient Cultural Story about the existence of a creature known as Satan is plainly and simply inaccurate.**

It is okay now to remove this ancient teaching from our current story, and to stop telling this to ourselves and to our children.

There is no such being as Satan, and hell does not exist.

Those who believe that Satan *does* exist assert that his non-existence is exactly what Satan himself would declare, and would attempt to get us to believe. Therefore, anyone who says that Satan does not exist is seen not simply as someone who has a theological difference with the religious mainstream, but, more ominously, as "an instrument of the Devil."

This ensures that such a difference of opinion is rarely revealed or widely discussed.

We will, nevertheless, discuss it here.

That which human beings *call* evil *does* exist in our reality, as part of the Contextual Field described earlier. Yet our definitions of "evil" are creations of our own devising, having nothing to do with any kind of inherent evil in God's Kingdom.

Indeed, it is the absence of "evil" in the realm of the spiritual that requires us to create it in the Contextual Field within the realm of the physical, so that we may express and experience what we call "good."

We do not have to create it on our own planet, however. So long as something that we label "evil" exists *somewhere* in the Contextual Field (which is the universe) we can experience that which we call "good." As well, we can use *memory* as a device with which to create a Contextual Field. Therefore, if we can remember a time when we experienced or heard about something "evil," we can in the present moment experience that which we call "good." Therefore, the presence and the expression or experience of "evil" on the earth today is not a requirement for the expression or experience of "good" to take place.

Because what we call "evil" is a creation of our own making does not mean that what we call "evil" is not "real" in our experience (insofar as anything within this illusion called physical life is "real"), or that labeling things, in human terms, as "good" and "evil" has no value.

Indeed, it is by what we ourselves call "evil" that our species defines itself—and those definitions change as the species itself evolves. Yet it is critically important for us to understand that those labels are *our own*, and have not been indelibly "stamped" on certain actions or conditions by either a Deity or a Devil.

I will now offer dramatic evidence that this is true.

*

On July 28, 1999, in a weekly address witnessed by more than 8,500 people, Pope John Paul II said that a physical, literal hell as a place of eternal fire and torment *did not exist.* Rather, the Pope said, a hell-like experience can be encountered by the soul—not only after death, but even in this life. This experience, the Pontiff said, was the experience of separation from joyful communion with God.

According to an official Vatican transcript of the Pope's speech, John Paul II noted that the scriptural references to hell and the images portrayed by them are only figurative and symbolic of "the complete frustration and emptiness of life without God."

He added, "Rather than a physical place, hell is the state of those who freely and definitively separate themselves from God, the source of all life and joy."

The Pope went on to say that the ancient notion of a hell of fire and brimstone, and the frightening images from some scriptures and other sources and paintings, are also only "symbolic." Such illustrations, he said, should not be used to scare people.

To cite his exact words: "The thought of hell and even less the improper use of biblical images must not create anxiety or despair."

The Pope also said that God does not condemn us to hell. Eternal damnation, he explained, is "not attributed to God's initiative, because in his merciful love he can only desire the salvation of the beings he created."

He did not explain why God cannot bring to fruition His "only desire," but did say that it is a human being himself who closes off to God's love. And so, damnation is actually a human being's own doing—the result of a free will choice to reject God and His forgiveness.

(For those who wish to look it up, the statement by Pope John Paul II was reported in the August 4, 1999 edition of *L'Osservatore Romano*, the newspaper of the Holy See. The Weekly Edition in English is published for the U.S. by The Cathedral Foundation, 320 Cathedral St., Baltimore, MD 21201. His remarks were also reported in the Religion News Service, a news agency reporting on religion, ethics, spirituality, and moral issues.)

And now, for that dramatic illustration of the similarities in the messages now being received and shared by human beings that I spoke of earlier . . . .

☼

The Pope's commentary bore a striking resemblance to the words of Christian evangelist Billy Graham in an interview conducted by a major news magazine some years ago. Asked about the eternal furnace of hell, he offered this:

> "The only thing I could say for sure is that hell means separation from God. We are separated from his light, from his fellowship. That is going to be hell . . . When it comes to a literal fire, I don't preach it because I'm not sure about it." *(Time* magazine, 11-15-93)

And . . . these utterances by both Pope John Paul II and Billy Graham not only resemble each other, but come remarkably close to the words found in the book *Home with God in a Life That Never Ends,* the final installment in the nine-text *Conversations with God* series.

Here is the dialogue from that source, beginning with words attributed to God:

> Let us be clear. Hell does not exist. There simply is no such place. Therefore, there is no such place for you to go.
>
> Now . . . can you CREATE a personal "hell" for yourself if you choose to, or if you believe this is what you "deserve"? Yes. So you can send your *self* to "hell," and that "hell" will turn out to be exactly as you imagine or feel a need for it to be—but you will not stay there for one moment longer than you choose to.

Who would choose to stay there at all?

You'd be surprised. A lot of people live within a belief system that says they are sinners and must be punished for their "offenses," and so they will actually stay in their illusion of "hell," thinking that this is what they deserve, that this is what they "have coming" to them, that this is what they *have to do.*

It will not matter, however, because they will not suffer at all. They will simply observe themselves from a detached distance and see what is going on—something like watching an instructional video.

The dialogue then says that the moment any soul wishes to get out of this self-imposed hell, that soul finds itself, at the speed of thought, in a place of unconditional love, total knowing, absolute joy, and complete emersion and union with God.

All of these statements—from the Pope, from Rev. Billy Graham, from *Home with God*, and from many other sources of contemporary spiritual wisdom who could also be quoted here (but will not be in the service of time and space)—completely contradict what the Bible writers said in ancient times about the reality of a literal lake of fire that burns throughout eternity.

Previously in this text I said that, as a *product* of evolution, "not just one or two of us, not just a few people, but millions everywhere are now receiving God's eternal message. It is coming through to humanity more ubiquitously and more accurately than ever."

I also said in that earlier statement: "Not coincidentally, nearly all of these 'new messages' contain similar statements, offer similar observations, provide similar answers, and describe similar realities."

So the question is, has the human race evolved sufficiently to finally move beyond the level of our earliest stories and statements about an Evil Spirit and a Place of Fire and Brimstone? Or shall we continue to refuse to question the Prior Assumption?

The statement should be made again that setting aside the notion of a Devil does not mean abandoning our notion that some things are "good" and some things are "evil," by humanity's current definition.

The trick is to not *meet* "evil" with "evil," but to realize that its very existence is a product of the Contextual Field which exists only in the realm of the physical, and thus to bless those who perpetrate "evil," even as we seek to change what they have done.

What's this?, you might say. *We are to bless evil-doers?*

Yes. Every spiritual master who has ever walked this planet has understood that. It is why all spiritual masters, each in their own way, have sent the same basic message to humanity: "Love your enemies. Bless them that curse you, do good to them that hate you, and pray for them which despitefully use you and persecute you."

Buddha said: "Even if thieves carve you limb from limb with a double-handed saw, if you make your mind hostile you are not following my teaching."

Those teachings flow to humanity to the present day. The Dalai Lama spoke this is the twenty-first century: "Hatred will not cease by hatred, but by love alone. This is the ancient law."

Can we believe the words of our spiritual masters? If they did not want us to believe them, why would they have said these things?

Could it be that they were trying to tell us that, through the highest expression of love, we could dissolve the pain and the power of everything and anything that we do not consider to be the most magnificent expression of love?

Could it be that every spiritual master has known that during all human lives we have been and are going to be invited to have the courage to contradict what most people would consider the "right" thing to do when under attack?

Does this mean that we should not respond when under attack? No, it does not mean that. But it does mean that the *way* in which we respond does not have to be the traditional way of self-defense and counter-attack, and can thus nullify the effects of the attack.

All love will in all ways nullify all negative effects of all attack. It may not alter the outward appearance, but it will forever alter the inward experience. And this, in turn, often *does* alter the outward appearance.

Nelson Mandela was imprisoned for twenty-seven years in South Africa, but he refused to condemn his jailors. On the contrary, he chose to openly love them. The result: the guards fought to be assigned to his area. They sought his counsel regarding their personal problems, and he sat patiently with them in his cell, offering his gentle advice. It is said that on the day that Nelson Mandela was released from prison, the guards wept. They had lost their best friend.

He understood at a very deep level that . . .

All love will in all ways nullify
all negative effects of all attack.

☀

It is when we realize that we have the power to neutralize not just an attack, but any negative energy in any form whatsoever—from minor annoyances to the day's major calamities—that we see that negativity itself is something we are subjectively producing, not objectively experiencing. We are creating it, not encountering it. It is in interior decision, not an exterior condition.

Our inner struggle around this interior decision regarding any exterior event, condition, situation, or circumstance is what every spiritual teacher, every saint and every sage has spoken of through the ages as the biggest challenge of being human. Many Muslims refer to this inner struggle as *jihad*.

There is no creature or being such as Satan. God did not create an angel and watch it turn into a Devil, then allow it to bedevil humans for the entirety of their existence. But God did give humans the power to see things in any way that they wished. It may be helpful to think of SATAN, then, as simply an acronym for: Seeing Any Thing As Negative.

Like Nelson Mandela, we can adopt any perspective on any aspect of life that we choose. Our perspective will then create our perception, our perception will create our belief, our belief will create our behavior, our behavior will create our experience, and our experience will create our reality.

The decision to see something, anything, as negative is a choice made by us, and only by us. There is no "evil spirit" who has power over us.

Or, as the comic strip character *Pogo*, created by the late cartoonist Walt Kelly, was noted for saying: "We have met the enemy, and he is us."

Another Misunderstanding about God: *God determines what is Right and Wrong*

We have already said that when it comes to deciding what is "good" and "evil," millions of people—indeed, entire societies and cultures—have used as their basis an understanding of what the God in whom they believe is said to have announced, declared, commanded, and demanded.

This is also true of the larger and more nuanced labels of right and wrong.

In the end, most of the world's people have taken it on faith that God is the defining and deciding authority regarding appropriate and inappropriate human behavior. Indeed, the *civil laws* of many countries and jurisdictions are rooted in this view.

Now comes The Great *What If* . . .

What if concepts such as right and wrong
do not even exist in the Mind of God?
What if there are no such delineations
or definitions in Ultimate Reality?

Would it make a difference? Does it matter? In the overall scheme of things, would it have any significant impact in our planetary experience?

Yes. And let us be clear. This goes past the simple, gross-motor-movement definitions of "good" and "evil." This gets down to the most delicate shadings of human thought, words, and behavior.

Billions of the world's people would suddenly be rudderless on what they have created to be a stormy sea of human experience without what they presume to be God's guidelines on what is right and wrong in many subtle areas. We pretty much know about "good" and "evil." But is, for instance, falling in love with the "wrong" person at the "wrong" time intrinsically "good" or "evil"? Is cheating on one's income tax "good" or "evil" if one believes that the government is using it for "bad" things?

People around the world now base much of their individual behavior, as well as the decisions and actions of their clan, group, or tribe, on the Prominent Public Pronouncements of their particular faith tradition about not just the gross motor movements (killing, stealing, etc.) but the more subtle, finer maneuverings of the body human (the little white lie, the discreet affair that presumably hurts no one, etc.).

For Jews and many Christians this Prominent Public Pronouncement is the Ten Commandments. For Muslims, it is the Five Pillars of Islam. For Buddhists, the Noble Eightfold Path and the Five Precepts. For Hindus, the Doctrine of the Fourfold End of Life. For those practicing Kemeticism (a reconstruction of ancient Egyptian religion) there are the 11 Laws. Members of the Bahá'í Faith follow the Kitáb-i-Aqdas (the book of laws of Bahá'u'lláh). Sikhism has the Reht Maryada.

This list goes on.

If suddenly it was made clear that God *has* no laws—that divinity's pronouncements and Deity's revelations contain no commandments, requirements, regulations, rules, instructions, guidelines, precepts, principles, criteria, or behavioral do's and don'ts of any kind—the rug would be pulled from under most of traditional theology, and not a small amount of global jurisprudence.

If standards for human conduct are *not* to be based on the demands of our Creator (for the reason that our Creator has *made* no demands), then our species will have to come up with a new rationale for declaring a certain action, choice, or decision "right," and another one "wrong."

If we take "morals"—i.e., the values arising out of our understanding of God's commands or desires—out of the picture, then the question arises: What shall be the Gold Standard for the deportment of our species?

One thing appears certain about our present standard: the arbitrary labeling of choices and actions as "right" and "wrong" based on seemingly capricious, often varying, and too frequently contradictory interpretations of God's Law has done more harm than good in far too many instances around the world for that standard to any longer be considered reasonable, or even useful, within an enlightened society.

Once again I refer to the 2014 sentencing of a person to death for her religious choices, as substantiated in Chapter Six, as a striking and immensely sad illustration of this. Yet the search for, and the creation of, a new behavioral standard could lead to massive upheaval in humanity's social and spiritual communities—which is no doubt why ancient standards are clung to.

Nobody wants to rock the boat. Not even when the boat is sinking.

Nobody wants to question the Prior Assumption.

GOD'S MESSAGE TO THE WORLD

God has been telling us from the very beginning, and it is becoming more clear to us every day, that **humanity's Ancient Cultural Story about right and wrong is plainly and simply inaccurate.**

It is okay now to remove this ancient teaching from our current story, and to stop telling this to ourselves and to our children.

In Ultimate Reality there is no such thing as right and wrong. These concepts are human constructions based on a massive misunderstanding of what God wants, and a total lack of comprehension regarding both the reason for, and the purpose of, life itself.

The reason that judgments about right and wrong are not present in the mind of God is that the concepts themselves are based on the condition or the experience of benefit and damage—neither of which exist in Ultimate Reality.

Nothing can be of benefit to That Which Is The Source Of All Benefit. Imagining that something benefits God is like imagining that a penny benefits a billionaire.

Nothing can damage That Which Is The Source Of All That Is. Imagining that something damages God is like imagining that an action story about a little boy who hurt himself and then got better is damaging to the author who wrote it.

Because God cannot be benefited or damaged in any way, the idea of something being right or wrong does not exist in the mind of God.

This idea will not exist in the mind of humans, either, when human beings come to understand that they, also, cannot be benefited or damaged in any way. This is so because human beings are not separate from God—a truth that we will look at in great depth when we explore the Final and Greatest Misunderstanding about God in Chapter 23.

For now, it may be useful to remember this:

Because God cannot be benefited
or damaged in any way,
the idea of something being
Right or Wrong does not exist
in the mind of God.

It is very possible for human beings to experience the *illusion* of benefit or damage during their physical experience upon the earth, yet this is but the result of their idea about what is occurring.

William Shakespeare put this another way: "There is nothing either good or bad, but thinking makes it so."

In other words, we are making it all up. We are defining and deciding what is "good" or "bad," "right" and "wrong," depending upon our mood of the moment, given the situation, time, and place.

In Peoria, Illinois prostitution is "wrong." In Amsterdam, The Netherlands it is a legitimate business, licensed and regulated by the government, and not a small source of tax revenue.

In 1914, living together out of wedlock was considered "wrong." In 2014 it is considered a good idea before entering into the long-term commitment of marriage, or for older folks seeking companionship in their later years without the legal entanglements of matrimony.

We are making things up as we go along, and we are changing our minds as we go along—yet we get caught up in any given moment imaging that, in this *particular* moment, what is right is right, and what is wrong is wrong.

God has nothing to do with these delineations. They are entirely a product of humanity's constructions. If God were defining right and wrong, those definitions would remain constant. What is true in Peoria would be true in Amsterdam. What was true in 1914 would be true in 2014. Right and wrong would not be determined by map or calendar.

☀

The question before humanity, then, is not whether God declares something to be right or wrong, but what is it that makes *a human being* do so?

The observable answer is that human beings have already decided (although few wish to admit it) that they are going to judge every one of their prospective choices or actions as being right or wrong *based on whether they believe it will be effective in achieving their goals.*

Thus, humans can sanction the state killing someone intentionally, even as humans declare that killing someone intentionally is wrong.

Thus, humans can cheer a Robin Hood tale of robbing from the rich to give to the poor, even as humans assert that stealing is wrong.

Thus, humans can convince themselves that a sexual encounter with another's mistreated and ignored spouse in the name of love is romantic and understandable, even as humans maintain that adultery is wrong.

In human interactions it turns out that nothing is considered right or wrong *absolutely*, but that these judgments are made within a particular *context.*

This is the truth of it on the earth. It would serve us to openly admit this, and then to decisively declare that our new Human Code of Conduct shall be based not on "morals," or what we have arbitrarily decided that *God* wants and commands, but rather, on *what works and what does not work, given what it is we are trying to do.*

If you are trying to win the motorcar race at the Indianapolis 500 Speedway, it would not be "wrong" to drive 175 miles an hour. If you are trying to get to the grocery store in your neighborhood without endangering yourself or others, you may not want to drive that fast. It simply does not work, given what it is you are trying to do. Indeed, there are no doubt traffic signs where you live making it clear that such behavior is prohibited.

There is difficulty and challenge in *openly acknowledging and utilizing* such a practical measure as the Gold Standard for human behavior, however. (Again, it must be made clear that we already use this standard—it's actually *built into our laws*—but we simply don't freely admit it.) The difficulty is that humanity would then have to admit to itself that our " Gold Standard" is all over the place, and thus, not a "standard" at all, because we, as a collective, are *profoundly unclear about what we are trying to do.*

(Example: It's not okay to "shoot first and ask questions later." Unless you call it a preemptive strike, using weapons of mass destruction to defend against another nation's weapons of mass destruction that, it turns out, were not even there. Or "stand your ground," in which case the thought that you might be in danger—even from having a bag of popcorn or a cell phone thrown in your face in a movie theatre (where, according to "the rules," you should not even be carrying a gun)—is sufficient defense in a Florida court of law for shooting and killing a man.)

This entire concept of moral "right" and moral "wrong" will be explored in crisp terms later in this text. Stay tuned for that. For now, know that our standards of behavior are all over the place because most of the members of our species are completely confused about Who We Are (our true identity as sentient beings) and Why We Are Here (the real reason for life, and the purpose of individual and collective experience).

And *this* is because humanity is totally mistaken about the reality, function, purpose, and nature of God.

Another Misunderstanding about God: *God's forgiveness is required for us to get into heaven*

Having used the criterion described above as a measure of whether an action or choice is right or wrong, but not wanting to *admit* that they have used it—and, worse yet, having no idea of what they are actually trying to do during their time upon the earth—many human beings are understandably worried about how God will judge them in light of what they are certain is a long list of transgressions.

Billions of humans find comfort, however, in the assurance of many religions that God will forgive even the worst offenses. A notable notion in the Jewish tradition is *teshuva*: the ability to repent and be forgiven by God. In Catholic doctrine, we are told about the sacrament of Confession. Other religions, as well, teach that God will forgive us.

Under certain conditions.

The trick is to know what the conditions are . . . and then, of course, to meet them.

Humans have turned to religion to tell them what those conditions are, yet what makes this tricky is that the conditions appear to shift from religion to religion. It has therefore become a matter of extreme importance and no little urgency to billions of people that they discover and belong to the *right religion*.

A mistake here could be monumentally hellish.

☼

Now comes The Great *What If*. . .

What if God will never forgive us
for anything? What if God considers
the whole concept of forgiveness
unnecessary?

Would it make a difference? Does it matter? In the overall scheme of things, would it have any significant impact in our planetary experience?

Yes. Of course it would. Forgiveness is one of the lynchpins of all faith traditions—and thus, of the moral code of most of human society. If forgiveness is out of place in human affairs (to say nothing of the affairs of God), then how can human beings ever expect to evolve beyond resentment and revenge?

Still, for all the emphasis placed by religion on forgiveness as a tool of healing and restoration, such evolutionary advancement has not been grandly evidenced. Indeed, in some respects our species seems to have *de*volved, not evolved. Resentment and revenge seem to mar the collective human experience today more than ever. Often, in fact, they dominate it.

Day after day, week after week, month after month the world's headlines are filled with stories of war, revolt, violent government crackdowns, individual hate crimes, shocking mass murders, jealous rages, vengeful lawsuits, vitriolic politics, hurtful break-ups, heartless cruelty, rancorous outbursts, and bitter behavior.

It seems clear that simple forgiveness is not stemming the tide. Something else, something more powerful, is going to be needed to halt the growing use of violence as a tool in the resolution of grievances and the curbing of the apparently insatiable human appetite for retribution.

Yet how can we be expected to rein in our desire for retribution and revenge when we are surrounded by religions whose very creed declares: *Vengeance is mine, sayeth the Lord . . .* ? Are we to restrain ourselves in ways that God Himself does not?

Would humanity's penchant for holding resentment and seeking revenge change if we were told that God never forgives us for anything, because God sees no *need* for forgiveness—and if it was explained why?

I think the answer to that question is obvious.

GOD'S MESSAGE TO THE WORLD

God has been telling us from the very beginning, and it is becoming more clear to us every day, that **humanity's Ancient Cultural Story about forgiveness is simply inaccurate.**

It is okay now to remove this ancient teaching from our current story, and to stop telling this to ourselves and to our children.

As we explore what has been revealed about this, we begin to see several previous elements of the total narrative offered on these pages creating a logic line that helps us to understand why God would send humanity the five-word message on the cover of this book.

Watch closely now as these pieces of the puzzle—comments and observations you've heard earlier—entwine even more closely, weaving into a pattern that reveals the foundation of a larger overall understanding.

We are invited now to notice that while forgiveness can be a wonderful tool during the time that one is residing at normally experienced human levels of consciousness, it can actually be an *obstacle to one's spiritual development.*

As soon as one wishes to rise above the most commonly experienced human levels of consciousness to a place of *higher* consciousness or *grander* awareness, the idea of "forgiveness" as a tool of growth and healing falls away almost at once. "Understanding" becomes the most effective and powerful tool.

God has told us: *Understanding replaces forgiveness in the mind of the Master.*

Our soul knows—and it has reminded us here—that we are each an Aspect and an Individuation of Divinity. Because this is true, our soul cannot be, and has never been, hurt, damaged, or injured in any way. So, we never have to forgive anyone for anything, as each experience in our life has done nothing but move us forward on our soul's evolutionary journey. Thus, every experience is a cause for gratitude and celebration.

And there is another reason that forgiveness is unnecessary.

Since we are all *collaborators* in the producing of our outward experience, none of us can be a victim, in the spiritual sense, in the story we are collectively co-creating. It may seem, in the human sense, that we are, but as our mind embraces the wisdom of our soul, we realize that we are no more the victim of our particular crucifixion than Christ was of his.

In the moment that we accept that we *are*, each of us, individuated expressions of The Divine, we realize as well that nothing can happen *to* us, and that everything must be happening *through* us.

We see that the whole of our experience on the earth is being co-created by the lot of us, in a collaborative process that serves the agenda of the Whole through the expression and the experience of its individuated parts.

We understand fully, as did Christ, why anything and everything has happened in our lives, out of our total comprehension of Who We Are, where we are, and why we are here on the earth, experiencing the realm of physicality.

We suddenly know the *reason* that others have entered our lives in particular ways—ways that we formerly might never have forgiven—because now we are no longer "looking through a glass darkly," but observing with the eyes of the soul. We know, at last, the soul's logic and the heavenly purpose in co-creating all that has occurred, is occurring, and ever will be occurring in our lives.

To make this clear: our lifetime will provide us with the experiences, events, people, situations, and circumstances ideally and collaboratively created *for* us *by* us as pathways to self-realization.

In the moment that the mind embraces the soul's knowing, we will see with startling, stunning clarity that all that has happened—every.single.thing.—has happened not always with our conscious collaborative agreement, but always at our mutual spiritual behest, in order that we might collectively create and encounter conditions allowing us to announce and declare, express and fulfill, experience and become Who We Really Are.

It is in these moments that God is "made flesh, and dwells among us."

⁂

There is even a third reason that forgiveness is out of place in the experience of those who understand—a reason to which we alluded earlier.

I asked before and I ask again: When that sweet little one knocks over the milk reaching in eagerness for the chocolate cake, or when that older brother tries to "cheat" his younger sibling out of an equal share of the cake, do we subject them to endless punishment? Of course not. We understand that children are just exactly that—*children*, incapable of fully comprehending their actions (or, often, even controlling them).

Once again, so that you will not forget: This is how God understands our minds, and it is how we are all invited to understand each other. Not just the children among us, but all of God's children, whatever their age.

⁂

Many people continue to insist that God is simply not forgiving of certain transgressions, and it is based on this intractability that we justify our own. Yet Is God not at least as compassionate and understanding with us as we are of our children? And does an eternal God, existing across billions and billions of years, not understand that human beings, with a history that covers not half a breath in the life of the cosmos, truly *are* children of the universe?

Surely, even if there is a need for divine justice in heaven (as many religions insist), God would take this into account as God calls *us* to account, no? Even human courts of law declare a person "innocent" by reason of diminished capacity. Is this too high a standard for our God?

⁂

So now we ask, with regard to forgiveness: Could it really be possible that we've simply gotten God all wrong?

What if it is *true* that there is nothing in the first instance that our species is "supposed" to do or not do, no matter what its "age" in the universe? What if it is *true* that God is an all-powerful being—in fact, the *Source* of all power—who needs and requires nothing from human beings? What if the last thing God needs is to seek some sort of retribution or impose some sort of punishment?

What if God desires only for us to be totally happy, fully expressed, and abundantly joyful in the experience of life? And what if God understands that, given our immaturity as a species, we are going to do things along the way that we are going to label mistakes—some of them, egregious mistakes?

Or, to put it simply: Could it be that God is at least as kind and caring, compassionate and loving, generous and understanding as our own grandparents?

Perhaps it would serve us all to hold this as our truth:

Understanding replaces
forgiveness in the
mind of the master.

⁂

The new spiritual outlook of our awakening species invites us to ask: What if we were not children of a Lesser God, but, in fact, children of the Most Gracious, Wonderful, Wise, Generous, and Unconditionally Loving God of our imagining?

This is the truth of it. This is the Ultimate Reality. Everything else is a story we have made up. God's forgiveness is not necessary, because God understands all of us—and all of our behaviors—perfectly. And God sees each of us and each of our behaviors as manifestations and demonstrations of life's evolutionary process.

There is nothing to forgive when a full understanding replaces a limited awareness of the process of evolution itself, and when that understanding arises from the deep comprehension that the unity of all life evolving in every form is the ultimate expression of divinity.

Another Misunderstanding about God: *God has a plan for us*

MUCH OF THE WORLD believes in a God who has a particular plan in mind for every human being. This is a God who is said to have handed out to each of us specific talents and attributes, equipping each of us to undertake particular missions, perform discrete functions, and fulfill distinct and disjunctive purposes over the course of our lives.

Our job is to figure out what that plan is, and then to follow that plan as well as we can. Or, at best, to "go with the plan" as it makes itself obvious through the events of our days and nights.

Now comes The Great *What If*. . .

What if God has no specific plan for any of us?
What if God has no preference in the matter
of how we live our lives, or what we do,
in the specific sense, with our days
from birth to death?

Would it make a difference? Does it matter? In the overall scheme of things, would it have any significant impact in our planetary experience?

Yes. First, it would relieve us of the burden of having to figure out what we are "supposed" to be doing here, and how. We could end our search, stop our pursuit, quit our quest, and conclude what we have constructed in our reality as our sacred seeking for God's sacred assignment.

Then, we could begin at last, in full awareness and in earnest, the journey upon which we really came to the earth to embark. This is not God's "plan," this is the soul's desire. And this always has to do with what we are *being*, not what we are *doing* in and with our lives.

If we thought that God did not have a specific agenda in mind for us, we could pay attention to what our life has to offer us in terms of beingness opportunities, rather than what we think God has planned on our behalf (either for beingness *or* doingness). And we would stop seeing certain occurrences, coincidences, and confluences as "a sign from God" that we can now move forward with "God's plan."

As well, if we thought there was no such *thing* as God's plan for us, we could drop many of the notions of religion, all the ideas of pre-destiny, and every imagining that a hidden agenda for us exists in divine mind, which God is simply not making obvious and clear to us (for reasons that are not evident).

We could also stop killing each other out of an idea that it is "God's plan" that a nation of "God's people" who believe in God and practice God's will in a particular way must exist upon the earth—even if it requires the killing of thousands of other people to create it.

GOD'S MESSAGE TO THE WORLD

God has been telling us from the very beginning, and it is becoming more clear to us every day, that **humanity's Ancient Cultural Story about God having a plan for us is plainly and simply inaccurate.**

It is okay now to remove this ancient teaching from our current story, and to stop telling this to ourselves and to our children.

If God had a particular plan for every human being on the earth—or, for that matter, for the human race as a collective—God would have made it known to us long ago.

God would have no reason not to tell you in crystal clear, specific, and direct terms what God's Plan for you is. Why would God devise a particular course of action for every single individual on the earth and then not reveal it to any of them?

And to those who say, "God *does* tell us what it is. We are just not *paying attention,*" is this an assertion that God *is* talking directly to each human being, and that we are simply not listening?

And there are larger questions as well. Why would God have a specific plan for every individual in the world in the first place? What divine purpose would this serve?

Would it not serve a greater divine purpose for God to simply supply the power and to provide the mechanism with which all sentient beings might decide, declare, express, and experience *for themselves* who they wish to be, instead of having to follow a plan set in place for each of them ahead of time?

There *is* a divine purpose being served by life. But a purpose is not a plan. A purpose is the *reason* we're going to do things. A plan is an outline of the things we're going to do.

This experience we are all having on the earth is not just a happenstance, not merely the latest in a million-year-old sequence of biological events. There is more going on here than simply the living out of physical life for no reason whatsoever except to complete a process that began for us without our involvement or agreement. And that purpose is much larger in scope than the mere encountering and living through a series of pre-planned occurrences.

The agenda of God is that all life forms in the physical realm express divinity. Each soul, as an Individuation of Divinity, has an eternity in which to do this, and an infinite number of ways to accomplish it.

The soul willfully and intentionally uses life in the physical as a means with which to express and experience all the aspects of divinity that it is possible to experience. These aspects are limitless, thus, life itself would have to be without end in order to experience them. And so it is.

Each separate physical expression of a soul's infinite life offers it an opportunity to select and express any aspect or aspects of its divine nature that it chooses. Thus, the soul comes to each lifetime with an agenda, but not with a plan. The soul's agenda may be to express and experience compassion, for instance, or patience and understanding. But the soul does not come to physical life with a predestined decision to do so by becoming a nurse, or by writing a book on human psychology.

To reiterate then, an agenda is the underlying intention or motive of a particular person or group. An agenda has to do with purpose. A plan has to do with process. It is a specific way to achieve a purpose, to follow through on intention. God and the soul have an agenda, but neither God nor the soul dictates or plans how a particular person should, or is going to, fulfill that agenda.

Thus, it is not "God's Plan" for a particular person to be in a car accident as a child, or experience the divorce of parents, or marry three times, or have no children, or have four children, or contract leukemia, or move to Nebraska, or become a famous painter, or meet just the right person at just the right time to move their career forward.

It is not "God's Plan" for one particular person to be a minister rather than a professional football player, or another to be the dynamic leader of a country rather than a dynamic country music star.

It *is* God's *agenda*, carried into the realm of the physical by the soul, for that soul to experience states of Being—the sum total of which equal the All that we call God. Or, as it was said just above:

The agenda of God is that
all life forms in the Physical Realm
express Divinity. Each Soul, as an Individuation
of Divinity, has an eternity in which to do this,
and an infinite number of ways in which it may be
accomplished.

What are these states of being that represent the many parts or aspects of God? With this as our soul's agenda, life invites us to be many things.

- Creative, for instance. Or compassionate.
- Understanding, for instance. Or patient.

- Helpful, for instance. Or generous.
- Loving, for instance. Or healing.

All of these are states of being. And these, plus many more, may be experienced in any moment of Evernow, individually or simultaneously.

Now you may think, "Is that *it?* It that all that life is about? I was hoping to actually *do* something. Something that really *mattered.* Something that *made a difference.* Something that contributed to others and to the world at large. Something that allowed me to feel fulfilled."

Yet that is precisely what the agenda of expressing and experiencing states of being is all about. When we examine life closely we realize that everything and anything we could do with our life is nothing more than an approach, a method, a process, an *impulse* that leads us into a state of *being.* Every thought, word, and action creates *beingness.* That is their only purpose. As *Conversations with God* says: *Every act is an act of self-definition.*

As to how you can know what *beingness* your soul has chosen, simply look to see what brings you the most joy. What impulse calls you? What feeling magnetizes you more than any other?

When you truly internalize this, your whole life can change. And the next step following such a realization is the awareness that what you hoped you would be able to *be* by *doing* a particular thing in a particular way, you can *be* in any *number* of ways.

And *that* becomes life's greatest freedom. The freedom from living as if a specific and particular kind of *doing* is *required* of you in your life in order for you to *be* what your soul deeply desires to *be.*

Now the road ahead is wide open. Now the path is yours to choose. Because you can *be* what you've chosen to *be* by doing anything—or by not doing anything at all. You can also decide to *change* what you choose to be, by simply changing your mind about that. And as you take the path that brings you the greatest joy, you can at last make a *life* rather than a *living*.

*

It is true that sometimes things seem to fall into place so perfectly in our lives that we are tempted to exclaim, "It's God's plan!" Or things may *not* work out the way we had hoped or imagined they would, and we may say, "God had other plans for me."

Such figures of speech reveal to us just how deeply the notion that God has specific ideas for each of our lives has seeped into our culture. It would be beneficial, however, not to let those figures of speech turn into actual, factual conclusions about "how things are." Otherwise, we will indeed be tempted to spend a huge amount of our time "trying to figure out how to figure out what God has figured out for us."

We'll measure every nuance, every energy, every event against whether we feel this is what God has in mind for us—all the while God has nothing in mind for us at all. Not in the sense of us being a "butcher, baker, or candlestick maker." Only in the sense of us using life to experience the highest and most joyful aspects of Who We Really Are and How We Choose to Be.

Indeed, the purpose of life *everywhere*, in *every* form, is to express divinity—physicality being the vehicle through which God experiences Itself as all that It knows Itself to be.

This is done through God differentiating Itself, then giving its multitudinous and magnificent parts the wherewithal to express life variously—but without specific instructions, directions, requirements, or plans of any kind for every individual expression.

⁂

Life forms in the cosmos have been imbued with varying levels of consciousness, or what might be called self-awareness. This inbuilt ability to *know oneself* as an Individuation of Divinity is present in all sentient beings, and is increasingly experienced by each such being through the process called evolution.

The evolving into the full experience and demonstration of Who We Are is the journey upon which every soul has embarked, and the completion of that journey is achieved in every moment in which our highest notion of divinity is expressed.

The process of life (as opposed to "the plan") is that we all simply *do* this, in whatever way we freely and spontaneously choose, given the possibilities to which we are daily opened by the collaborative creation of all the souls co-creating with us.

Completion of the soul's journey is, therefore, not something that is experienced once, but over and over again throughout the ongoing manifestation that is life itself—now and eternally.

There can be what seems like a down side to this for many people. Humans feel more comfortable when they feel guided. They like to be instructed, directed, *told* what to do. As an emerging species, this is their proclivity. Like children, they feel safe when clear boundaries are drawn, and specific commands or orders are given. Then all they have to do is *meet the requirements* and they're home free. This accounts for the immense popularity of religion. It allows humans to follow their deep inner impulse toward The Divine *without having to figure out how to do it.*

It is therefore a disappointment to some people to learn that God has no plan for us, no instructions to give us, no guidelines we must follow, and no commands to heed. It can be at once both freeing and frightening to realize that God's agenda is for *us* to *decide* who we wish to be and how we wish to demonstrate that, not spend our life trying to figure out *how* to figure out what *God* has figured out for *us*.

Yet God is like the master teacher in an art class. The best art teachers do not tell budding artists, "Here is your canvas. Use this next hour to create. Oh, but make sure that there is maroon and a big splotch of orange in the picture, and be certain to place the orange in the upper right-hand corner. Also, I need to see a three-dimensional effect, and there have to be children in the foreground and a telephone somewhere."

The master teacher knows that the purpose of education is not to put something *into* the student, but to draw something *out;* not to instruct, but to extract. And so the master teacher simply places before the student all the implements—all the crayons, sketch pencils, brushes, oil paints, watercolors, and dyes—needed to work in any medium, then says with a smile, "Joyously create!"

"But what if I don't get it right?" the timid pupil cries.

"There's no way *not* to get it 'right,'" the master teacher assures. "*This is art!*"

Another Misunderstanding about God: *God honors self-sacrifice, long-suffering (preferably in silence), and martyrdom*

THERE IS AN IDEA about God, shared by many, many people in the world, that God is pleased when human beings make a personal sacrifice—and that the bigger the sacrifice, the more pleased God is.

God's pleasure, we are told, comes from knowing that we are "putting others first," even in the face of great personal emotional, physical, or financial loss.

In addition, God is said to reward the long-suffering—particularly when we suffer in silence. Complaining about some circumstance or condition besmirches and lessens the value that has been gained through the suffering itself. So to gain optimal value in heaven, keep your suffering to yourself. That's been the basic message.

When I was a child, the nuns in our parochial school told us, if we fell and got hurt, to "offer it up to God."

Martyrdom in any form was, we were taught, the highest form of suffering, for which we were accorded a special place in heaven. And martyrdom for *God* was the highest of the highest, garnering the greatest reward: sainthood.

I am not the only person to have gotten these messages. They have lived long, primarily (but not exclusively) in the Christian tradition.

✵

Now comes The Great *What If . . .*

What if God does not offer a special
reward in heaven for any particular
behavior—and, in fact, wants us to know
that self-sacrifice and suffering do not have
to be part of the human experience?

Would it make a difference? Does it matter? In the overall scheme of things, would it have any significant impact in our planetary experience?

Yes, it surely would. Billions of people across the globe would stop seeing self-sacrifice and long-suffering as qualifications for the highest honors in heaven.

This shift in understanding would eliminate an enormous amount of human sadness and loss produced by self-induced behaviors generated by people who think that they are pleasing God by displeasing themselves.

In addition, invalidating "martyrdom for God" as "automatic passage" into heaven would mean that ending one's life in order to kill scores of innocent people would lose its spiritual *credentials*—making it impossible for the trainers of terrorists to promise young male suicide bombers that they will be rewarded with everlasting joy and twenty-two black-eyed virgins in paradise if they will just go out and blow themselves up in public places.

The biggest change that would occur if humans were certain that self-sacrifice, long-suffering, and martyrdom not only brought no special reward from God, but that God says that none of this even needs to be part of the human experience, is that people would begin to ask, "Why, then, is it so normal?"

The answer to that question is so huge that, if it were shared and lived widely, it would transform life for our species forever.

GOD'S MESSAGE TO THE WORLD

God has been telling us from the very beginning, and it is becoming more clear to us every day, that **humanity's Ancient Cultural Story about God according higher honors to the soul for self-sacrifice, long-suffering, and martyrdom is plainly and simply inaccurate.**

It is okay now to remove this ancient teaching from our current story, and to stop telling this to ourselves and to our children.

Self-sacrifice is never necessary, suffering need not be a common part of human life, and martyrdom "for God" does not earn anyone a special place or the highest honors in paradise.

What is called "self-sacrifice" is the result of an assessment by a human being that something they are choosing to do is producing loss or self-injury in some way.

What is called "suffering" is the direct result of an assessment by a human being that something they are experiencing they should not be experiencing.

What is called "martyrdom for God" is the result of an assessment by a human being that something they are doing that is producing enormous self-injury (perhaps even death) pleases God *because of this*, and will therefore generate rewards in heaven proportionate to, and in recompense for, the injury experienced on the earth.

All of these assessments are inaccurate.

Looking at these concepts one by one, we see that it may be perfectly normal within our present human understanding to think that when one is doing something for another at great inconvenience, and especially at great emotional, physical, or financial loss, one is "sacrificing the self for another." Yet such a mental holding is both inaccurate and self-serving.

Yes, rather than self-sacrificing, it is *self-serving*.

The truth is that no one does anything they don't want to do. It sometimes serves us, however, to do exactly what we want to do, and then to tell ourselves (and others) that we "had no choice," or that we did it "at great personal sacrifice." In this way, we can feel self-satisfied and victimized at the same time.

Everything that human beings do willfully they do at their own choice, of their own volition. It is true that some people feel that certain things *have* to be done, or that there really *is* no choice when one is under duress—and within the context of humanity's extremely limited comprehension, such a view might be understandable. But in reality, even "duress" is just a fancy word meaning "a situation in which I am confronted with a condition I do not consciously desire, or an outcome that—for my own good reasons— I seek to avoid."

Yet when you consciously sidestep a condition you do not desire, you are serving yourself. And if you seek to avoid something for your own good reasons, then when you avoid it you are once again clearly serving yourself. This does not mean that your reasons are not *good*, it merely means that the goodness of your reasons does not make them less self-serving. Indeed, *just the opposite is true.*

(The better is your reason for doing or not doing something, the more self-serving it is—obviously.)

Yet we have been trained to think that anything that is self-serving is "bad," and so we would much rather say that we "had no choice" than to say that we indeed had a choice, and took the option that we chose because it felt best to us—and thus, *served* us.

Even the decision to do something for another at great personal inconvenience or loss falls into that category, or you can be assured that it wouldn't be done. There is some *reason* that a person makes the decision to do something extraordinary for another, even at their own expense or risk.

Perhaps the reason is that it makes them feel good. Perhaps the reason is that it brings them a direct experience of the kind of person they see themselves being, or wish to be. Perhaps the reason is that it allows them to feel true to a life principle they've committed to live by, or to an obligation they genuinely feel, or to a promise they have made.

All of these reasons, and many more that one could come up with, serve the ultimate interest of the self. *And there is nothing wrong with this.* What is not beneficial is serving the self, then telling oneself (and others) that one is not doing so.

We see, then, that true self-sacrifice is not possible, but *faux* self-sacrifice *is*, within the limited framework of most human understanding. Yet our larger awareness—the awareness of the Soul—tells us exactly why we do everything . . . and the reason *always* serves the agenda of the doer, thus is always self-serving. Further, it *ought to be.* It is *intended to be.* For the purpose of life itself is to allow us to "show up" in every moment as the grandest version of the greatest vision ever we held about Who We Are.

When we become clear about this we eliminate the possibility of harboring anger or resentment toward anyone else regarding anything we have ever done for them, may now be doing, or may think that we "have to do."

We can no longer feel victimized by another, nor even by our own choices, but are invited to claim our place as the powerful sentient being that we are, clearly seeing all the options and outcomes before us in any given moment, and clearly choosing the ones that we see serving us in the best way.

What we may be missing here—an insight that would turn everything around for us if we saw it clearly—is that all self-service is service to the whole. It may take a deeper level of thinking for all members of a species to "get" this, but all members of all species eventually do. Ultimately, at a certain point in the evolutionary development of a species, this becomes crystal clear:

All self-service is service to the whole.

There are multiple reasons this is true, as will become apparent before this narrative is concluded.

☀

The lens of humanity's understanding is clouded, at best, and totally obscured in our worst moments, due to the extraordinarily young age of our species (to review this understanding, refer back to Chapter 11). Our immaturity is revealed and demonstrated when, upon encountering severe physical or emotional pain, we feel that "this should not be happening," and that its occurrence is somehow a "violation" of the human contract.

A reversal of this single assessment can eliminate "suffering" from the human experience. While such a change of mind does not erase the pain, it transmutes it, turning it into something that can be encountered with a higher degree of even peaceful acceptance, and certainly with a great deal less—if any—objection or opposition.

It is objection or opposition that creates the brittle rigidity that produces suffering—and prolongs it. For it is as *Conversations with God* tells us: What you resist, persists, and what you look at, disappears. That is, it ceases to have its illusory form.

A classic example of this can be a woman in childbirth. She is in pain, but if she relinquishes any opposition to it, she can reduce—and often completely eliminate—"suffering." She can even, by this device, *reduce the pain itself.*

There are those who understand this very well, and who see pain as a natural part of every birthing process. Not just the birthing of a baby, but even the emerging of a new and greater aspect of the Self.

In children we often call these experiences "growing pains." They are precisely the same in adults.

Fair enough, some may concede, but must these "growing pains" continue throughout one's entire life? Is there to be no relief, *ever*, from this ongoing and ever-visited experience? Is the human journey to be an endless rush through tiny valleys of happiness to the next mountain of physical or emotional pain?

No. It does not need to be this way. Tiny valleys of happiness can turn into expansive plains of joy. The scales of life need not be heavily tipped toward emotional or physical discomfort—and even if certain physical pain is chronic, the abandonment or prohibition of joy is not a required accompaniment to that condition.

Many people who experience chronic physical pain have nevertheless found joy and happiness to be the prevalent circumstance of their life. Persons encountering ongoing emotional pain have likewise discovered that there are effective ways to ameliorate that condition and that they need not automatically forfeit delight, pleasure, and merriment in their lives.

It is quite amazing to observe the degree to which a non-combative, non-oppositional attitude toward pain can begin to immunize a person to the worst ravages of it. A person's subjective, or inner, decision can and does affect a person's objective, or outer, experience. There is not a psychologist in the world who would disagree with that.

Metaphysics goes one step further. It says that a person's interior holding of an event can actually *change the event itself.* In other words, a positive attitude about any negative occurrence can actually transmogrify the occurrence itself—*even as it is occurring.*

How is this possible?

It is possible because everything in life is energy. And *energy affects energy.* It is a phenomenon that impacts upon itself. Science observes this through quantum physics, which posits, as we noted earlier, that *nothing that is observed in unaffected by the observer.*

This is pure science, not hocus-pocus.

So let's highlight this intriguing statement once again here, so that you can get the full impact of it:

A person's subjective, or inner, decision
can and does affect
a person's objective, or outer, experience.

It is within this context that the statement is made that long-suffering need not be part of the human condition. Not only does God not specifically reward it, God promises that it is not even necessary.

As well, it should be made clear that affecting one's own happiness in an irreversible way—to say nothing of ending one's life—through an act that is labeled "martyrdom for God" is not something for which God offers a special reward. The act of taking the lives of others along with one's own as the very point of such "martyrdom" likewise will not, and will never, be rewarded with special honors or special treatment in paradise.

Persons who imagine that by killing themselves in an act of terrorism that kills others they will earn a unique, distinct, and exclusive "payoff" in the afterlife will find that no such unique payoff is waiting.

Unlike on the earth, everyone is treated exactly alike in heaven. No one is raised higher, nor placed lower, than anyone else, no matter what they have or have not done during their physical life, and the wonders of the afterlife are not merit awards that are earned.

To put this simply: heaven is not a meritocracy. The joys of the spiritual realm—as with the joys of the physical realm—are the gifts of life itself, joyously created and freely given to all by God.

☀

The doctrine of a God who parcels out rewards in heaven based on the quality and the content of one's "performance" on the earth reduces the whole of life's magnificent process to the monotonous mechanics of a mundane meritocracy.

As well, such a dogma makes a muddle of the concept of reincarnation, for if one's particular status in heaven is a "reward" for exemplary behavior on the earth, that status would have to be revised with each succeeding incarnation—raising the almost silly question: Does one's "standing" go up or down based on the "achievements" or "failures" of one's most recent physicalization?

No.

Heaven is not a meritocracy.

It is time to let go of our notion of a God who admires, honors, and rewards self-sacrifice more than self-service, long-suffering more than lifelong joy, and martyrdom more than merry-making.

We have lived long enough with our childish concept of a God who has gone so far as to say that even music and dancing is "bad," that sex without the intention of procreation is lustful and bestial, that glorious self-celebration is worth less than continuous self-denial, and that the foregoing of some of the grandest joys of our oh-so-short life on the earth is what earns us the grandest joys of everlasting life in paradise.

We have lived long enough with our childish idea of a God who lays down "rules" for human behavior that dictate what we may or may not eat, may or may not wear, may or may not say, and may or may not believe. These jejune and puerile theological constructions have nothing to do with Ultimate Reality.

Or, as one observer wryly put it: "No more Jonah and the Whale."

Another Misunderstanding about God: *God sometimes answers our prayers and sometimes does not*

MUCH OF THE WORLD believes in a God who hears our prayers and sometimes gives us what we ask for and sometimes does not.

This conception of Deity holds that God has *reasons* for granting or denying our wishes on any particular occasion.

Sometimes (so it is said) what we want for ourselves is not what God knows is "good for us," so we don't get it.

Sometimes (so it is said) we have sinned so much that God does not find us "deserving" of having a prayer answered.

Sometimes (so we are told) God gives us all that we have asked for and more—presumably because it *is* good for us and we *are* deserving.

Now comes The Great *What If . . .*

What if God does not grant or deny the prayers of anyone?

What if a hoped-for event or condition manifests in our life for another reason entirely?

Would it make a difference? Does it matter? In the overall scheme of things, would it have any significant impact in our planetary experience?

Yes. This would, in fact, offer an opportunity for the biggest breakthrough in human history. We could at last discover, as a global species, the Process of Creation and the alchemy of the universe (a seemingly magical method of transformation or creation).

If we thought there was another reason that one particular outcome rather than another manifests in our lives—a reason having *nothing whatsoever* to do with our worthiness or the worthiness of our request—it would end our seemingly endless and far too often ruthless drive to please God so that He will answer our prayers. As well, it would launch a worldwide effort to discover what that reason *is.*

Why *do* hoped-for events or conditions manifest in our lives if it's not God's "mood" that determines whether our wishes are granted? How do miracles happen? What makes dreams come true? And what is at cause when they do not?

If humans thought that God does not grant or deny the prayers of anyone, but that God has simply and lovingly put into place a *process* for manifestation that does not rely on us being in God's "good graces" or our request being "good for us," many humans would no doubt stop praying.

What would be the point of it, they might think, if asking God for what we want and need is not a way to produce it? And so this would be a second reason humanity would put an end to Supplication Theology, replacing it with Application

Theology—*applying* the power of God in our lives, rather than *supplicating* for it to be applied in our lives.

If our species decided *en masse* that God does not personally grant or deny prayers, but, rather, has given all of us a mechanism by which all of our desires may be made manifest, religions themselves would be dramatically affected. Some might even disappear. Those that remained would see their missions significantly altered. They would still present themselves as pathways to peace, joy, and paradise, but they would provide insight into how such experiences may be called *forth* rather than called *for.* (The latter is a request, the former is a requisition. There is a huge difference.)

Yet if prayers of supplication were to disappear, something would have to come along to replace them as a tool with which to generate hoped-for results as humans faced the day-to-day challenges of life on the earth. And something *would* come along.

The truth.

GOD'S MESSAGE TO THE WORLD

God has been telling us from the very beginning, and it is becoming more clear to us every day, that **humanity's Ancient Cultural Story about God personally granting or denying the prayers of individual human beings is plainly and simply inaccurate.**

It is okay now to remove this ancient teaching from our current story, and to stop telling this to ourselves and to our children.

God's role in our lives need not be reduced, however. Indeed, it would be well to *increase* it. Yet if God does not personally say "yes" or "no" to our prayers, why bother increasing God's role in our lives?

Because it is God's *power*, not God's *disposition* that produces the manifestation of a human being's desires.

That sentence is important enough to qualify as one to be highlighted.

It is God's power, not God's disposition,
that produces the manifestation
of a human being's desires.

What this means is that it is not whether we are in God's favor, or whether or not God thinks that granting a particular request would be "good" for us, that determines the outcome of our prayer. It is not God's mood, it is God's love which produces the astonishing circumstance of *all of our prayers being granted all of the time.*

The problem is not that God sometimes says yes and sometimes says no to our prayers, the problem is that we don't know what "prayer" *is.*

If someone had told us when we were little children what prayer *is,* we would find that *all* of our prayers are answered all the time.

Prayer is an application, not a supplication . . . and most of us think it is the other way around.

Prayer is nothing more than God's energy, *focused.* Of course, if you don't believe in God, it could be psychologically more difficult to focus God's energy. That is why it was said earlier that you may want to make God more a part of your life—even as you make prayer, in the old style of supplication, less.

God's energy is not made available to us only under certain conditions (as when God agrees with our prayer, or when we are in God's "good graces"). God's energy lives *in* us, *as* us, and manifests *through* us every hour of every day, whether we know it or not—and whether we want it to or not.

We don't have any choice about this, because God's energy—which is the power behind creation—is not turn-on-able and turn-off-able. It is *always* on, every single moment. It is, in fact, Who We Are.

We are, each of us, a manifestation of God's energy, and how we *use* the energy that we *are* determines how we experience the life that we live.

All of this will begin to come together if we continue to revisit this statement: Life itself is nothing more than energy, vibrating at particular and various frequencies. Energy vibrating at certain frequencies produces physical manifestations in the form of objects, situations, circumstances, and events. This occurs because energy attracts energy. Energy impacts upon energy. Two energies produce a third energy. And so it goes, throughout all of life.

Remember always . . .

We are a manifestation of God's energy,
and how we use *the energy that we* are
determines how we experience the life
that we live.

Let me offer here what I explained in a passage from the book *Happier Than God.* The attracting aspect of energy responds not only to what we desire, but also to what we fear. Not only to what we wish to draw *to* us, but also to what we wish to push away. Not only to what we consciously choose, but also to what we unconsciously select.

"Selecting" from what my friend Deepak Chopra calls "the Field of Infinite Possibilities" is a delicate procedure. It is a matter of what we focus on, *whether we want to or not*, whether we do it *consciously or not.*

For instance, if your mind is focused on doubling your income within the next year, but if you have a later thought, the next hour or the next day, that it will be almost impossible for you to do this—if you say to yourself, "Oh, come on, be practical! Pick a goal that you can at least *reach*"—then you have selected the latest idea, *whether you originally wanted to or not*, because the switch on your power is always ON; personal creation is always working.

It not only works with your most recent thought or idea, but also with the one to which you give the most frequency and focus and emotional energy.

This explains why some people who seek to use the so-called Law of Attraction or traditional forms of prayer to get something they desperately want often meet up with what they call failure. Then they say, "See? This stuff doesn't work!"

Actually, the process is working perfectly. If you experience yourself wanting something desperately, and if you keep saying to yourself *I want that!*, you are announcing to the universe that you do not now have it.

(Unless you are simply using the word "want" as a figure of speech. Most people are not. When most people say that they "want" something, they are very clear that it is because they experience that they do not now have it.)

As long as you hold such a thought, you *cannot* have it, because you cannot experience on the one hand what you are confirming on the other that you do *not.*

To use one example, the statement, "I want more money" may not draw money to you, but may actually push it away.

This is because the universe has only one response in its vocabulary: "Yes."

It responds to your *energy.* It listens most of all *to what you are feeling.*

If you constantly say, "I want more money!", God will say, "Yes, you do!" If you think, "I want more love in my life!", God will say "Yes, you do!"

The universe "feels your energy" around the question of money or love, or anything else for that matter, and if it is a feeling of lack, *this is what the universe will respond to.* And it will *produce more of that.* The universe is a big copying machine. It duplicates what's put into it.

We are talking about *power* here. We are talking about the power of prayer. But prayer is more than simply what we ask for. Prayer is our every thought, word, and deed. In fact, asking for something is actually the weakest path toward getting it, because asking for something is an affirmation that *you do not now have it.*

Putting all this another way, your energy has the power of a magnet. Remember that even feeling (actually, *especially* feeling) is energy, and in the matter of energy, Like Attracts Like.

The idea is to step into the application of the power of God, not a supplication to God that the power be used. God's invitation is to utilize the confirmative power of prayer. How? How is this done? Well, here's an example: "*Thank you God for sending me my perfect mate.*" Here's another example: "*All the money I need is coming to me now.*" And here's my favorite prayer: "*Thank you, God, for helping me to understand that this problem has already been solved for me.*"

This shift from supplication to application can be miraculous. These are not affirmations. These are *confirmations.* There is a huge difference. An affirmation seeks to produce an outcome or an experience. A confirmation announces that the outcome has already been produced.

⁂

On the very day that I was putting together this chapter I received the following email in my box in response to an article I had written on this subject.

"Dear Neale," the letter said, "I have a difficult time believing that God/my soul is so literal regarding 'wanting.' Doesn't God/my soul know what I really mean/intend? God bless, Gerry."

I wrote back:

> Dear Gerry . . . It is not a question of God, or your soul, being so "literal" regarding "wanting." It is a question of how the Mechanism of Creation *works.*
>
> This *is* a *mechanism* we are talking about here, not a Being in the sky who takes you literally or does not. This is a *machine* that runs based on the fuel that is put into it. It is a copying machine, and it has no preference as to what it duplicates. Nor does it try to *interpret* what its owner wants to make copies of. It simply duplicates the energy that is put into it. In this sense, it is like a computer. You've heard this acronym, I'm sure: GIGO. That stands for: *Garbage In, Garbage Out.*
>
> One of the great misunderstandings that humans hold about God is that God has a preference in the matter of how life is experienced by each of us. God loves us, for sure, but God has no such preference—any more than you have a preference as to whether your children pay "tag" or "hide-and-seek" when they go out to the backyard. All you

want them to know is that you are there if they need you. And so it is with God.

There are seven billion sentient beings on this planet—and this planet is one of seventy trillion-billion planets in the cosmos. To functionalize this breathtakingly expansive life God has put into place a spectacular apparatus, and its workings have nothing to do with Deity's personal preference. They have to do with Deity's genius.

The genius of the system is that it is Pure Energy, reacting to Energy by reproducing in physical form what is put into it by all sentient beings in the form of their thoughts, words, and actions—which, in turn, are based on what humans call "feelings" . . . which, in turn, are simply other forms of energy.

Do you get the picture?

God does not answer some prayers and fail to answer others. God answers *all* prayers, sending to The Collective the Energy that duplicates what The Collective is thinking/saying/doing/feeling. God does so, as well, on an individual basis with each source of energy output. (That is, with every human being, and every sentient creature in the universe.)

Is this quite remarkable? Yes. Is it the result of God's personal preference in the matter of what is manifest moment-to-moment in the cosmos? No.

☼

In using God's Energy, the word "I" is the ignition key of creation. What follows the word "I" *turns* the key and starts the engine of manifestation.

Thus, when it "looks as if" Personal Creation is not working it is only because the Primal Energy has brought you what you *inadvertently selected* rather than what you thought you chose.

If the power were not always ON, if the process was not always working, you could have a single very positive thought about something and that outcome would be made manifest in your reality without fail. But the process works all the time, not just part of the time, and is fed by that which you feel most deeply, most consistently. So a single very positive thought in a whirlwind of not-so-positive ideas and projections is not likely to produce the desired result.

The trick is to stay positive in a sea of negativity. The trick is to know that the process is working even when it *looks as if* it is not. The trick is to "judge not by appearances." The trick is to stay in the space of gratitude for everyone outcome and experience, every circumstance and situation.

Gratitude eliminates negativity, disappointment, resentment, and anger. And when those emotions disappear, room is made for the energy of love for God, for life, and for yourself to reappear—now more fully than ever.

What a God we have! What a Deity is ours, to have created such a foolproof, magnificent, miraculous process, allowing each of us to announce and declare, express and fulfill, experience and become Who We Really Are.

Another Misunderstanding about God: *God is on our side*

One of the most common ideas about God is that God is on our side. God is in our corner. God grants *us* favors because we are in *God's* favor.

We have told ourselves that when we go to war, God is on our side. When we kill thousands of people in acts of terrorism, God is on our side. When we struggle to make our religion the dominant religion across the face of the earth, God is on our side. When we create a new country, God is on our side. When we attempt to tear apart an old country, God is on our side. When we launch a social, political, or economic revolution, God is on our side.

And especially when we seek to defend ourselves, God is on our side—which is why all attack is called a defense. Have you ever noticed that? Nobody ever says they are attacking anybody. All attacks are called defensive, and are thusly justified.

☼

God is on our side in positive matters, too. We've told ourselves that we were successful in an election campaign because God is on our side. We landed that huge contract because God is on our side. We got to the wedding on time, even though there was a huge traffic jam, because God is on our side.

Wait, it gets even more trivial than that. We kicked the winning goal in the World Cup because God is on our side. We hit the home run in the bottom of the ninth because God is on our side.

(We round first and head to second pointing a victorious index finger to the sky to let everyone *know* that God is responsible for the feat. We drop to one knee and make the Sign of the Cross after catching a touchdown pass to make it clear that we praise and thank God for our success.)

God cares who wins the game.

That's the message, loud and clear.

God cares.

God cares whether the pass in the end zone is complete or incomplete. God cares whether you hit a home run or strike out. God cares whether you get the most votes or do not. God is on your side, not the other side. If God were on the *other* side, *they* would win. If God were on *everyone's* side, it would be a draw. Every game would end a tie. Every effort would be a stalemate.

Fortunately, it isn't that way. God wants *your* side to win the war. God wants *your* idea to make thousands of dollars. God wants *your* parking space to be there waiting for you.

Yes, the message is clear. And each of us can say it without seeing any contradiction. *God is on our side.*

⁂

Now comes The Great *What If*...

What if God is not on anybody's *"side"?*
What if God does not care who "wins,"
who "loses," who's "right," who's "wrong."
who "succeeds," who "fails," or who does
or does not do anything at all?

Would it make a difference? Does it matter? In the overall scheme of things, would it have any significant impact in our planetary experience?

Yes, obviously it would. Right now, billions of people are *sure* that God is on their side—and there could be no more dangerous thought than that.

This idea has given rise to more actions that have caused more misery for more people than almost any other single notion. The spiritual arrogance of the idea is ignored by most, who seem to want to sidestep the obvious conclusion that if God is on their side, then God, *in fact*, must not be on the other side.

This sets God up as a Deity who chooses winners and losers, declares ideas worthy or unworthy, labels decisions fair or unfair, pronounces countries good or evil, designates religions right or wrong, calls people saved or condemned, and holds all manner of preferences and priorities, proclivities and predilections, penchants and partialities.

And, of course, if God is on our side, then God's preferences and priorities, proclivities and predilections, penchants and partialities all agree with ours.

GOD'S MESSAGE TO THE WORLD

God has been telling us from the very beginning, and it is becoming more clear to us every day, that **humanity's Ancient**

Cultural Story about God being on our side is plainly and simply inaccurate.

It is okay now to remove this ancient teaching from our current story, and to stop telling this to ourselves and to our children.

It is important to understand that God was not made in the image and likeness of man. It is the other way around. Man is made in the image and likeness of God.

It would be wonderful if this could be placed on billboards around the world:

God was not made in the
image and likeness of Man.
It is the other way around.

This means that human beings are divine, each having all the qualities of divinity within them. What it does *not* mean is that God has human qualities. So God does not like the Los Angeles Dodgers better than the Atlanta Braves. And God doesn't want your country to win the World Cup more than God wants another country to win it.

God is not hoping that your nation is victorious in the war rather than the nation you are fighting. And God does not support the world's revolutionaries more than God supports the world's governments. And God does not align with the values of the Republican Party more than God aligns with the values of the Democratic Party.

It's time for human beings to let go of their need to believe in a God of preferences. First, we had to let go of our God of the brand name, now we add to that list our God of preferences.

Derailing some really fundamental ideas embraced by many people, it is time to accept the fact that God does not hold the thought that women should never be priests or members of the clergy, that gays should never be allowed to be married, or that non-Christians should never be allowed into heaven.

Difficult as it may be for some people to imagine, God does not, we repeat here for emphasis, prefer Baptists over Hindus, Catholics over Jews, Muslims over Mormons, or any religion over any other religion. God does not even prefer those who believe in God over those who do not believe in God.

These are not God's ideas. These are the ideas of human beings who *think* that these are God's ideas.

We said it before and we'll say it again: God is not a male human being writ large. God is the Supreme Intelligence and the Primal Energy underlying the universe . . . an intelligence and an energy without specific identity.

Is it really conceivable that God has a favorite color or a favorite number, a favorite team or a favorite player, a favorite nation or a favorite religion, a favorite gender or a favorite race?

Does it feel realistic that God holds particular political views, or economic views, or social views, or spiritual views? And if so, *which ones?*

Wait. We don't have to ask that. The people who hold particular views will tell you which ones. Theirs, *of course.*

Well . . . while this disrupts the whole story line of people and political parties and nations and religions wanting to insist that they are the lone upholders of moral values and the last bastions of spiritual rectitude on the earth, it is important that humanity come to clarity on the true nature of divinity and the factual aspects of Ultimate Reality.

None of the above means that *life* is against us. God is not on our side in the sense that God favors you over someone else, but *life* is always prepared to give us what we most fervently and feelingly believe we are going to receive.

Life proceeds out of your intentions for it. We have been told, "As you believe, so will it be done unto you," and that is true. *Belief* is a strong and very powerful energy. It is a magnet. It attracts to us what we firmly expect it to. Yet this is not because "God is on our side"; this is because God has given us, as described earlier, a mechanism with which to manipulate and affect the raw energy that is All of Life.

Life affects life through the process of life itself. The Essential Essence is an energy that has an impact upon Itself.

One who learns how to use this energy in a positive fashion through thought, word, and action has stepped onto the road to mastery in living.

Yet never "pray" or use the power of thought, word, and action to bring you something to the detriment of another. Always remember, there is only One of Us.

If, therefore, you seek something for yourself to the detriment of another, you "win" with the right hand and "lose" with the left. Even if you seem to have "won" in one instance, the experience of how you "lost" will visit you in the next.

When in any sort of situation where your desires are juxtaposed with another's, say a prayer, or hold the thought, that the outcome that is produced will be the one that is *best for all concerned.*

This is true spiritual mastery, for it requires and demands nothing, but holds every outcome and experience as perfect. In this awareness is found both freedom and peace.

Another Misunderstanding about God: *God will reward us or punish us on Judgment Day*

We are seeing again how the many misunderstandings about God string together, one emerging from another and birthing a third. That is why you are seeing so much repetition in this text. It is not so much repetition as extension. It is the extension of a Logic Line.

The notion that God will reward or punish us on Judgment Day is the part of the logic line that starts with the idea that we are required to fear God, continues with the doctrine of a God at war with the Devil, expands with our notion that God's forgiveness is required for us to get into heaven, and eventually reaches the intersection described above, where God will reward or punish us on Judgment Day.

Many religions teach us—based on all the previous misunderstandings—that about this Judgment Day: a time when God will reward or punish us, based on "how well we did" in our lifetime.

As challenging as this may seem for many people, it is particularly onerous for people who believe that they have only one lifetime in which to "get it right"—and then find themselves surrounded by a hundred different people giving them a hundred different ways in which to do it.

⁂

Now comes The Great *What If . . .*

What if God does not judge us, ever,
and there is no such thing as
Eternal Reward in heaven or
Everlasting Punishment in hell?

Would it make a difference? Does it matter? In the overall scheme of things, would it have any significant impact in our planetary experience?

Yes. Certainly it would. Among other things, it would remove the motivation for countless decisions, big and small, taken by countless people over countless moments in countless lifetimes.

Most of the world's population makes most of its choices based on the desire to "do what is right," and therefore be "right with God," and therefore go "right to heaven" when life on the earth is over.

Even people who have done what most human beings feel is "wrong" have convinced themselves it is "right" because it is "what God wants," and therefore, it will earn them a place in paradise.

Suffering a long and painful death is one example of this. Causing *others* to suffer a long and painful death is another. Denying oneself some of the simplest pleasures of life is a third example of this. Denying *others* these pleasures is a fourth. And this list goes on.

And on.

And on.

Further, if humans thought that God will not judge them for anything at any time, they would, as we have noted previously, lose the spiritual grounds and the moral authority to judge others.

And finally—again as we have noted before—humanity would have to find some other measure by which to determine what it finds acceptable and unacceptable behavior by members of the species.

In short, a God without judgment would overturn the applecart of humanity's entire value system, requiring it to find *another reason altogether* to reward some behaviors and punish others. Truly advanced civilizations would eliminate punishment completely from their social systems.

Consequences would replace punishments in societies that stopped trying to encourage certain behaviors or discourage others with punitive measures.

GOD'S MESSAGE TO THE WORLD

God has been telling us from the very beginning, and it is becoming more clear to us every day, that **humanity's Ancient Cultural Story about God rewarding us with eternal life in heaven or everlasting punishment in hell is plainly and simply inaccurate.**

It is okay now to remove this ancient teaching from our current story, and to stop telling this to ourselves and to our children.

We live in a cause-and-effect universe, not a reward-and-punishment universe.

God does not keep a running list of all the misdeeds of all the people in all the places on all the planets through all the ages, then dock points from a perfect score, and finally, if a person's score falls below a certain level, cast souls into hell as soon as they arrive on The Other Side.

That simply isn't how it works.

As has been made clear here now a number of times, there is no "hell" for God to cast people into—and God wouldn't have a reason to do so even if there were.

God—the Source of Supreme and Unlimited Intelligence, and of Unending and Unconditional Love—is simply and joyfully witnessing the process of evolution proceed across the trillions of star systems in the cosmos, placing in the hands of intelligent beings everywhere the same mechanisms, the same tools, the same instruments and powers of creation, then giving all of those life forms free will to determine how they wish to use their divine ability, both individually and collectively, in the manifestation of their experience.

There is, without question, a system and a process in the universe facilitating, empowering, and governing with supreme sophistication and utter perfection all physical life functioning. One could loosely call this The Law, or even God's Law, in the same sense that we use the phrase "the law of gravity." The Law is simply *how things work*. It is the process by which pure energy is—

—what is the word to use here . . . ?—

—*manipulated*. . . . in order to produce in the physical realm particular and specific manifestations, as discussed at the close of the previous chapter. This Law provides the soul with the opportunity to create particular and specific expressions, bringing the total being (i.e., body, mind, and soul) particular and specific experiences. Namely, experiences of its true identity. That is, experiences of divinity.

Just as The Law can be used to produce the highest experience of the Self, so, too, can it be used to produce what, in the judgment of some sentient beings, has been called the lowest.

Earlier we said that the power is always on, and so sometimes is used in ways that generate inadvertent results. To help humans understand this, let's use the example of atomic energy here. This is an illustration that has often been used.

Atomic energy is neither "good" nor "bad," nor does it have inherently within it a predilection or a desire to be used in a particular way. It simply IS. It exists in a state of utter neutrality, and may be used in any way that the sentient beings manipulating the energy intend to use it.

The energy itself does not "punish" the user of it, based on how the energy itself is manipulated. The user experiences the *results* according to his *use*, and *that* is the *consequence*—which is neither a "punishment" nor a "reward."

It is as simple as that.

It is as elegantly and ingeniously simple as that.

There is nothing complicated about the process of creation. It is really very simple. Listen to your soul. Create your wish list while you move through life, based on the soul's innermost desire. Call it forth and receive what arrives with gratitude that perfection is manifest in every moment.

Herein is true peace truly found. It is the peace of which we have been told, and which we have been promised. It is the peace that passeth all understanding.

The American composer Leonard Bernstein captured the essence of the remarkably simple process of personal creation, gifted to all sentient beings by a remarkably simple God, when he wrote in the lyric line of the opening song for his extraordinary theatre piece, *Mass* . . .

Sing God a simple song, lauda laude.
Make it up as you go along, lauda laude.
Sing like you like to sing, God loves all simple things.
For God is the simplest of all.
For God is the simplest of all.

Another Misunderstanding about God: *God wants us to return to Heaven*

MOST OF THE STORIES that we are told about God tell us that God's wish is that every soul returns to heaven. As noted here earlier, Pope John Paul II said as recently as 1999 that it is not God who keeps us out of paradise, "because in his merciful love he can only desire the salvation of the beings he created."

Statements such as this from the world's most visible spiritual leaders instill in humanity a deep-seated feeling that God wants us all to return to rejoin God, and to experience the wonder and the perfection, the beauty and the glory of paradise, in eternal joy forever and ever, and even forever more. And we all have a chance to do so, if we'd only *obey the rules.*

Now comes The Great *What If*. . .

What if God does not want us to return to heaven? What if there is another way to *understand life—and another agenda for life—that had nothing to do with returning to heaven?*

Would it make a difference? Does it matter? In the overall scheme of things, would it have any significant impact in our planetary experience?

Yes. Good heavens, *yes.* This would change everything! If humanity's understanding of the very purpose for life is inaccurate, then the billions of people who believe in God and in heaven have no idea what they're doing here.

Sadly, for a huge number of people both statements are true. Humanity's understanding of the very purpose for life *is* inaccurate, and we as human beings *have* no idea what we're doing here. This is true, certainly, for the majority of humans.

I'm going to say, for the *vast* majority.

When we discussed whether it is God who labels things "right" and "wrong," we noted that the difficulty in creating a new standard for human behavior based instead on "what works and what does not work, given what it is humans are trying to do," is that humanity would have to admit to itself, at last, that as a collective, we *are profoundly unclear about what it is we are trying to do.*

This is the reason that very little of what we *are* doing is working.

We began this entire exploration with a cataloguing of the undeniable truth that our political system, our economic system, and all the other systems we have put it into place on this planet are not producing the outcomes for which they were designed. Worst of all, we noted, our *spiritual* system—which was supposed to solve all the *rest* of this—has actually *added* to our problems.

And why is that last sentence true? Because of what we think we have to do in order to be "saved."

Don't look now, but our history has shown that in our religious zeal, *we've been killing each other trying to save each other.*

What's enormously sad about this is that so many of us haven't even *thought* that it's enormously sad.

We've thought, through all the centuries (up to and including yesterday), that we were *doing God's work.*

For the 300 years of the Christian Crusades, during which people had their heads lopped off by the thousands if they refused to confess in Christ, people thought they were *doing God's work.*

For all the centuries that Muslims have sought to conquer and subdue entire countries, killing people right and left in order to create a caliphate, or Nation of Islam, people thought they were *doing God's work.*

During all the fighting and killing between Protestants and Catholics in Ireland, during all the fighting and killing between Sunnis and Shiites in Iraq, people have thought they've been *defending the faith* and *fighting for God.*

In conflicts ranging from social protests and civil rights battles to all-out war (such as the ongoing battle between the mostly Buddhist Sinhalese majority and the Hindu Tamil in the Indian subcontinent, to cite yet one more example), people have thought they are *fighting to protect their way of life and their beliefs.*

All of which led the Rt. Rev. William E. Swing, retired Episcopal Bishop of California, to poignantly and plaintively ask in the year 2000, when he founded the United Religions Initiative: "In God's name, can we stop the killing in God name?"

⁂

To be fair, most of us are not engaging in such activities. Far and away the largest number of the world's people understand that this cannot possibly be the way Home to a loving God.

So . . . billions of us are clear about what *not* to do, but billions of us are *un*clear about what *to* do.

We think that God wants us to get back to heaven, and we'll doing anything to help God get us there . . . including denying ourselves pleasure, refusing to eat certain foods, forcing ourselves to wear certain clothes, prohibiting ourselves from listening to certain music (and in some cases, *any* music), stopping ourselves from dancing, requiring ourselves to grow a beard, and refraining from any sexual activity whatsoever.

I am not making this up.

This, many of us have told ourselves, is the pathway to heavenly glory.

The trick for many has been trying to figure out how to *integrate* the behaviors necessary to get to heaven with behaviors necessary to get by on the earth.

Does one thing have anything to do with the other? We talked about this briefly in our examination of whether we are required to worship God in a certain way.

Should we be going to Mass every Sunday and on every Holy Day of Obligation, as do Catholics?

Should we be responding when the *adhān* (Arabic: أذان) is called out by a *muezzin* from the mosque five times a day, traditionally from the minaret, as do Muslims summoned for mandatory (*fard*) worship (*salat*)?

Should we be bowing at four points in the *Amidah*: at the beginning and end of both the first blessing of *Avot* and the second to last blessing of *Hoda'ah*, at the opening words of

Avot and at the conclusion of both these blessings, as in the Jewish tradition?

And what of those Ten Commandments, and the Five Pillars of Islam? What about the Noble Eightfold Path of Buddhism and the Doctrine of the Fourfold End of Life from the Hindu tradition?

Are we to obey the 11 Divine Laws of Kemeticism? Or the Kitáb-i-Aqdas, the book of laws of Bahá'u'lláh? And shall we adhere to, or simply ignore, the Reht Maryada, from Sikhism?

"Good heavens, God," we call out in puzzlement, "how do we get *back to You?* If this is what You want, why don't You tell us *how to do it* in one simple, clear statement?

Those are the questions that humanity has been asking for centuries.

No, for *millennia.*

And still, after thousands of years, the people who have populated this planet have not for one single minute in all of recorded history been able to agree on what God is answering in return. To this day we move in different directions—and fight with each other over which way is the right way to achieve this goal of returning to heaven.

Could it be that this is because that is not what we are supposed to be doing? Could it be that what we say we are trying to do on the earth has nothing to do with what we actually came here to do?

Could it be that, after all, there *is* something we do not fully understand about God, the understanding of which would change everything?

I believe the answer is yes.

I believe it is *obviously* yes.

There is *clearly* something about which we are *not clear*.

The question is, can we admit it? Or are our egos so big, so huge, that we cannot for one single second even explore the idea that there *may be something more to know on this subject?*

This is the central inquiry facing all of humanity in the first half of the twenty-first century. This is the critical question. We have reached a pivotal moment. Our species has come to a climacteric intersection.

GOD'S MESSAGE TO THE WORLD

God has been telling us from the very beginning, and it is becoming more clear to us every day, that **humanity's Ancient Cultural Story about God's wanting us to get back to heaven is plainly and simply inaccurate.**

It is okay now to remove this ancient teaching from our current story, and to stop telling this to ourselves and to our children.

God does not want you to get back to heaven; God wants you to know that you are in heaven *now*. God wants you to know that you never *left* the Kingdom of God. This kingdom is divided into three parts: The realm of the Spiritual, the realm of the Physical, and the realm of Pure Being.

Just as the Kingdom of God is divided into three parts, so, too, are you. The individuation of the Essential Essence that you have come to call "you" is made up of body, mind, and soul.

During your eternal lifetime what you have come to call your soul knows all three realms simultaneously. What you *experience* is the realm on which what you have come to call your mind focuses its attention. Thus, you may experience what you refer to as "life" or what you refer to as the "afterlife" or what you call "nirvana," "bliss," or "reunion with God."

Depending on which of these states you focus your attention on, what you have come to call your body emits certain characteristics, or what could be labeled energy signatures—or, more popularly, "vibes." In other words, your body—the corporate aspect of your divine self—alters the vibrational frequency of the Essential Essence to produce a Singularization of The Singularity. You are literally recreating yourself anew in every golden moment of Now. Certain religions call this being born again.

It is through this Individuation of Divinity in three parts, and it continual transmogrification, that the whole of divinity comes to know, express, and experience itself in its totality.

In this, as in all things, the Whole is greater than the sum of its parts.

Put in simple language, humanity (and all of life) is God expressing and experiencing Itself. Human beings are the individuations of divinity in particular form. We have called ourselves, not inappropriately, Children of God. We are, quite literally, God's issue.

Does anyone have an issue with that? I hope not, because we are all God's children, and we exist in God's paradise to experience the wonder and the glory of divinity. We do not experience this on the earth when we forget Who We Really Are.

Every human does so. The question is, *Why?* What does this serve? Why are we having this earthly experience, and what does it serve for us to forget our true identity?

We want to believe that God wants us in heaven, but if that is so, we ask, why would God continue to send us *here?*

Some have answered the question—some who accept the notion of reincarnation have replied—by saying that our multiple lives are designed to purify ourselves, so that we *can* return to God in heaven. It is almost as if *this* is our purgatory; *this* is our trial by fire. We get to go Home, we get to finally be "released" from the tribulations of physical life, when we have paid back our "karmic debts" and managed to at last live a life sufficiently free of human faults and foibles not to create any new ones.

Those who do not believe in reincarnation say that we come here only once, but that all souls must go through the process of this single lifetime because . . .

. . . well, we don't *know* why, actually. We don't even know how we got here (we understand the biology, but we don't understand the theology).

All we know is that we've found ourselves here through no choice of our own (or, at least, that's what it seems like to us), and we don't know what we're trying to do now that we're here—except to get *back* to where we think/hope/imagine we came from.

Where, pray tell, *did* we come from? What, pray tell, *is* the purpose of life? Is it to do whatever it takes to make sure we have a good afterlife? Is *that* what's going on?

No. That is not the purpose of life.

Our behavior on the earth has nothing to do with our admissibility to heaven.

I know, I know . . . I understand. That's almost a blasphemous statement. Certainly it amounts to one of the most radical, upheaving assertions that human theological excursions could encounter. Perhaps that alone compels its exploration.

Let us, then, repeat the sentence, and highlight it with deserving focus:

Your behavior on Earth
has nothing to do with
your admissibility to Heaven.

This is true not because God welcomes you back into God's arms after your life on the earth, no matter what. This is true because God doesn't have to welcome back into God's arms someone who has never left.

You are in God's arms *always*. Even now.

Yes, right now.

God has never let go of you. God has never turned from you, never not been there for you, never walked away from you—and certainly never pushed you away, burdening you with ancestral sin.

Your soul knows all of this. It is your mind which has forgotten, and for a very good reason.

The mind's forgetfulness allows the soul's remembrance to be experienced once again—and for the blissfulness of that remembering to be *re-experience-able eternally.*

When you find your beloved, you do not join in the wonder of making love only once. Nay, you embrace and part from the embrace, then embrace once again, knowing the bliss of reunion that can only be created by the parting.

This is true on a human level, and it is true on a celestial level. We are all remembering—or experiencing, once again, being *a member* of the Body of God.

Your soul always experiences being in the arms of God. It is experiencing this right now. It experiences that it is *part* of God, *one* with God. Yet your mind can cause you to think that this is not true, that it is not real. This is part of the mind's *job.*

The mind's task is to *differentiate* you in your experience from the Totality of You that is called God. This allows you to do what you differentiated in *order* to do—which is to experience the undifferentiated reality of You once again, one element, one aspect, one facet, one quality at a time. You are given countless lifetimes in which to do this, and countless opportunities within each lifetime.

⁂

Our Ancient Cultural Story says virtually nothing about this actual life purpose. It says many things that we have made up out of thin air, that have arisen out of myths and tales, legends and superstitions, that we've constructed out of our fears of what could happen if we were wrong, but it tells us nothing of our true purpose.

For centuries and millennia what elders have taught their progeny has been limited in this way. Right up to this very day, the old are teaching the young *the same old story*. Thus, "the sins of the fathers have been visited upon the sons, even unto the seventh generation."

This does not mean that we have inherited sins, it means that we have inherited *errors*.

A fundamentally challenging aspect of the human condition is not that we have all been "born in sin," but that we have been *taught* by those who have been *taught* by those who have been *taught* by those who have been *taught* something that is simply not true about Who We Are and Why We Are Here.

It is this misinformation that causes humans to act, to this day, the way we do. It is not our *nature*, it is our *instruction*.

⁂

So now, here, you have been given new instruction.

This is not the only place it has been made available to you. It is one of many places and multiple ways, and from every place comes the same message:

You did not come here merely to struggle to find a way return to where you came from. You did not arrive on the earth to simply try to get back to heaven. You never *left* heaven. Physical life is part of your everlasting life. You came to the earth to *experience* your Self as Who You Really Are, and you can only do this in the Kingdom of God—which is *where* you are *right now*.

There *is* another agenda for life, and it has nothing to do with you saving yourself. It has to do with you remembering yourself.

Your presence in the Kingdom of God has nothing to do with how "deserving" you are. God's love is not something that is *earned*. It is a given. And it is given to everything that is alive. Your being alive is evidence of it having been given, for life itself is God's Love, expressed.

Your presence in the Kingdom of God likewise has nothing to do with "justice." You did not get here because you did nothing wrong, or because you "paid for" any "wrong" that you did. The whole idea of "justice" as a rationale supporting the dogma of hell and damnation is explored *from God's point of view* in Chapter 24 of this text. It is something you will want to read again and again, for it lays bare the illusion of "justice" and "morality" with absolute clarity.

For now, we close our list of misunderstandings about God with a look at the biggest error of all.

The Final, and Biggest, Misunderstanding about God: *God is separate from us*

NOW WE COME DOWN to it. Now we encounter the *ultimate misunderstanding*, and give ourselves, at last, the opportunity to replace it with the ultimate awareness.

Most of us on the earth—those of us who have received some kind of religious training, and those of us who have come across the idea of God from simply moving through the world—have heard that God is the Alpha and the Omega, the All In All, the Beginning and the End.

We have also been told—in somewhat of a contradiction—that God is separate from us (which would make God *not* "the All in All"), and that our job, our task, our challenge is to somehow join together that which has been put asunder.

Now comes The Greatest *What If* Of All . . .

What if God is not separate
from us at all, nor separate
from anything *in any way?*

Would it make a difference? Does it matter? In the overall scheme of things, would it have any significant impact in our planetary experience?

Yes. It would change everything about the way life is lived upon the earth. It would change everything about the way you experience your Self. It would change everything about the way you experience each other. It would change everything about the way you experience God.

It would change everything about just about everything.

If our species accepted its unity with divinity, it would alter human behavior 180 degrees, for we would see every other being as blesséd, and perceive everything we are thinking or doing as something we are thinking about, or doing to, God.

If this was our perspective, we would not be *motivated* to think or do anything negative regarding anyone, for the simple reason that when every person treats every other person as divine, all the behaviors that would justify a negative response would disappear from the human experience.

Imagine how you would treat God if God were standing in front of you. Now carry that over to your human encounters and imagine how you would treat everybody else if you held them as divine. And imagine a world in which everyone treated you as if *you* were divine. In such a word, would you not treat them in the same way?

☀

Right now we seem unable to get to this place. We do not appear to be able to accept the notion on this planet that each of us is divine. This is in no small measure because most of those who embrace any kind of theology at all, embrace a Separation Theology.

A Separation Theology is a way of looking at God that insists that we are "over here" and that God is "over there."

This might be workable if that is as far as it went, but the problem with a Separation Theology is that it produces a Separation Cosmology. That is, a way of looking at all of life that says that everything is separate from everything else.

This might be workable if that is as far as it went, but the problem is that a Separation Cosmology produces a Separation Psychology. That is, a psychological profile that places "me" over here and "you" over there.

This might be workable if that is as far as it went, but the problem is that a Separation Psychology produces a Separation Sociology. That is, a way of socializing with each other that encourages all of human society to act as separate entities serving their own separate interests.

Even this might be workable if that is as far as it went, but the problem is that a Separation Sociology produces a Separation Pathology. That is, *pathological behaviors of self-destruction*, engaged in individually and collectively, and producing suffering, conflict, violence, and death by our own hands—as evidenced everywhere on our planet throughout human history.

The elimination of the Story of Separation from our Cultural Story would eliminate the behaviors that this ongoing saga has generated.

☼

The Story of Separation had its origin in the first attempts of our species to understand the life we were experiencing.

What we now call "self-consciousness" arose when we began to see or know ourselves individually. Perhaps it was seeing our reflection in a cave side pool that sparked this perception. We raised a hand to scratch our head and saw the "man in the pool" doing the same thing . . . and soon we began to conceive of "The Self."

The next step in producing the perception of separation came, perhaps, as we sat around the campfire of our clan and found ourselves startled by a sudden flash of lightning in the night sky, followed by a booming clap of thunder. We looked anxiously around the campfire and asked, with whatever facial and verbal expressions we'd developed, "Did *you* do that?" When everyone in the clan shook their head in a panicked "No!," we came to a startling awareness: *There is something Other Than Us.*

This Something Other also seemed, as subsequent events appeared to prove, far more *powerful* than us. It could cause wind and rain and violent storms; heat and dry spells that lasted, it seemed, forever; a frightening shaking and even an opening of the very ground on which we walked. It could even start fires in the woods all by itself.

It became clear to us that we needed to find a way to *control* this Something Other, or our lives would forever be at Its mercy. Yet we could not conceive of or imagine a way that we could do this. We tried everything. We knew we had to find a way to appease the gods.

We didn't call these elements of life "gods," of course. That word came along at a much later time. But we did think of this Something Other as an aspect of our existence that was both powerful and uncontrollable.

We knew some members of our own clan in exactly the same way.

The biggest and the strongest and most brutish member of the clan ran rampant through the collective life of the others, and efforts were continually made to appease him. He was brought offerings of every kind, from beautiful virgins to plentiful food to stunning things from the richness of the earth.

Once, when the most brutish among us became more sullen and angry than usual because of an unending drought and the sacrifices it imposed upon him, we joined others in our small group to do whatever we could think of to calm him, lest he take out his anger on us—which he had done before.

We threw a fireside "party" for the leader of the clan, singing and dancing for him. Someone in the group tore a dying branch from a nearby tree and shook it as part of his dance, its dry leaves making a rhythmic sound matching the dancer's gyrations as he twirled around the sputtering flames.

As it happens, at that exact moment the skies opened up, and a sudden hard rain drenched the site. Everyone was shocked! And, given the limited intellectual development of the clan at that time, the Dance with the Branch was credited with having produced the water from the sky.

A way had been found to please and appease Something Other! Not only was the brutish leader of the clan mollified, but the brutish Something Other was as well! Something Other was doing what we had been hoping for!

Everyone in the clan was so excited! The "rain man" was elevated to a position of highest status. Ritual, and a class within the clan of those who performed it, was created.

Because the clan believed that the Dance with the Branch by the Rain Man created rain, so it *did* in the *future* more often than not. Metaphysics being was it is, the formula worked. For the metaphysical process—whether modern or ancient—produces in physicality whatever it is fervently believed that it will.

In that first instance, the coincidental effect of the rain arriving while the dance was being performed was not produced deliberately, with intention. Yet it was no doubt the ongoing fervent hope, the deeply earnest wish, that the drought would end and that the leader of the clan would be mollified, which generated the rain. And the timing of the rain falling at the exact moment the noisy dance was performed could not be ignored. The two were put together as Cause and Effect.

Thus was religion born.

❋

The narrative above is all of my imagining. It was an insight—call it an inspiration, if you choose—that I received at the time of my own conversations with God. The entire story could be inaccurate, but I believe that either this, or something very similar to it, is what occurred in the early life of human beings, and is what produced our sense of separation, our sense of Something Other, and our sense that there might be, after all, a way of controlling—or at least *influencing*—this Something Other.

Earliest humans were dealing with the alchemy of the universe without knowing it. As we became more sophisticated in our understandings, our species began calling all of this activity "religion," as it explored and created more sophisticated ways of seeking to appease "the gods" . . . and, later, the single God that humans ultimately decided must surely exist.

We were right about that. There *is* the thing we now call God. Yet our fundamental idea of God—that it is "Something Other"—is what has been inaccurate.

GOD'S MESSAGE TO THE WORLD

God has been telling us from the very beginning, and it is becoming more clear to us every day, that **humanity's Ancient Cultural Story about separation is plainly and simply inaccurate.**

It is okay now to remove this ancient teaching from our current story, and to stop telling this to ourselves and to our children.

Just as the idea of a Devil is a myth, so too is separation a myth.

All things are One Thing. There is only One Thing, and all things are part of the One Thing there is.

The One Thing there is has been given many names by many people. Among them: Adonai, Allah, Brahman, Divinity, Divine Mother, Elohim, God, Hari, Jehovah, Krishna, Lord, Rama, Vishnu, and Yahweh. This is not a complete list.

Within the context of the present discussion this One Thing is called God. There is no one name that is the only, right, or proper name for the One Thing there is.

The One Thing may also be called, simply: Life. For life in all its manifest forms is what The One Thing is. All that is physical or non-physical, seen or unseen, known or unknown, is part of life, and, hence, is the manifestation of The Totality that is here called God.

Because the Essential Essence is the Only Thing there *is*, there is nothing else *but* The Totality—or God.

That, in fact, was the very *message* of the man called Jesus Christ. He came here to give us back to ourselves. He actually *said so.* He actually said that We Are All One. Let those who have ears to hear, listen . . .

"And for their sakes I sanctify myself
that they also might be sanctified through the truth.
Neither pray I for these alone, but for them also

which shall believe on me through their word;
That they all may be one; as thou, Father, art in me,
and I in thee, that they also may be one in us:
that the world may believe that thou hast sent me.
And the glory which thou gavest me, I have given them;
that they may be one, even as we are one."
(John 17:19-20)

But it was not only Jesus who is quoted in the Bible as making our true identity clear.

Have we not all one father? Has not one God created us?
Why then are we faithless to one another,
profaning the covenant of our fathers?
(Malachi 2:10)

. . . so we, though many, are one body in Christ,
and individually members one of another.
(Romans 12:5)

Because there is one bread,
we who are many are one body.
(1 Corinthians 10:17)

God exists in its Total Form forever, and can in no way, at no time, and by no cause or means be separated from Itself. If anything that exists were separate in any way from any other thing, the One Thing would then be more than One Thing—which is impossible.

While God exists as a singular reality, it is capable of manifesting in multiple forms. This multiplicity of *forms* should not be confused with a multiplicity of *things*. God is a single thing, revealing, demonstrating, and displaying Itself in endless variation. This is accomplished through a process referred to in human language as differentiation—a term was have used before in this narrative.

Differentiation is not separation, but simply individuation—even as the fingers of a human being are differentiated, but not separated, from the hand. Even as a stem cell in the human body differentiates, but is never *other than*, the cell itself.

Since there is only one element and one energy that exists, we can conclude and deduce that everything we observe and experience in physicality is an expression of that Essential Essence. This single element is the purest, undifferentiated energy that we call life. It displays and demonstrates itself everywhere we look—and, indeed, exists in the unseen as well.

The Essential Essence gives rise to an endless variety of life forms. These life forms are to God as waves are to the ocean: intrinsically part of It, demonstrating as singular expressions of It.

A wave in the middle of the ocean is not "other than" the ocean, nor does it need to "go back" to the ocean. It *is* the ocean, manifesting in specific form.

So, too, are you a part of God. You do not need to "get back" to God, you need merely to remember that you never were, and can never be, separated from God, and then to begin acting as if this were true.

As we have noted above, if all of humanity did this, our experience on this planet would become a miracle of love expressed, and our lives would never again be the same.

⁕

Of all the misunderstandings about God, this is the one with the greatest consequence. This is the one allowing us to feel alone, isolated, desperate. This is the one sponsoring hopelessness and despair. This is the one permitting cruelty, excusing revenge, absolving violence. Of all the misunderstandings about God, this is the one that makes all the dominoes fall.

Embracing the truth that God and we are One changes everything. It dramatically alters our entire experience of life. It radically shifts our day-to-day expression. It moves to a new level the whole of our birth-to-death encounter, opening us to an entire new way of being upon the earth.

We become, *in fact*, human beings, not humans doing—and when what we are choosing to be is divine, all the world that we touch is uplifted. For to be divine is to be love, plain and simple, and it is this for which our world yearns.

From the beginning of time all human beings have ever wanted was to love and be loved. And from the beginning of time all we have ever done is create rules and regulations, guidelines and traditions, tribal taboos, social customs, and religious prohibitions telling us who, what, when, where, why, and how we may love—and who, what, when, where, why, and how we may not.

Sadly, the second list is longer than the first.

This says something about us as a species. Not something bad, just something factual. It says what I have been saying here all along—that we are very young. Yet we are maturing.

We are.

And we are coming to understand that life is not what we thought it was, but a great deal more. And that God is not who we think God is. Not even close.

Now that we are done at last, finished forever, with our misunderstandings about God, we can get on with the joyous and exciting remembering of the Original Message.

Something We've Left Hanging

OKAY, THAT'S IT. Those are the major misunderstandings about God that I observe billions of people are clinging to, and those are my best articulations of the messages first given to me in *Conversations with God* having to do with those misunderstandings.

I hope I have done them justice, because I believe this information to be some of the most important knowledge that could be shared with our species at this time.

And speaking of justice, and of things important, it seems fitting that we move now beyond the misunderstandings to this idea of "God's Justice."

This is a doctrine that undergirds and supports the idea held by so many that we must be forgiven by God for our misdeeds, that we must "pay" for our sins through abject suffering in some midway stopping point on our way to heaven, or that if we have committed any totally unforgiveable sins, we will never be allowed into heaven at all.

All of these ideas are based on the notion that "divine justice" requires divine punishment of any of God's divine children who have acted in a way that is not divine.

This doctrine, promulgated by many religions, is meant to eliminate the confusion that is created when the traditional definition of our Deity as a "loving God" is coupled with the warning that we must nevertheless fear God.

The religions of the world could hardly place before humanity a doctrine of a Deity who is judgmental, vengeful, and ready to turn love to wrath without that Deity having a reason to do so—so religions came *up* with a reason. It was not lack of *love* that drove God to these actions, they said, but the need for *justice.*

Given this, our religions have told us, we should be able to understand why judgment without appeal, condemnation without exception, and punishment without end are necessary responses from God to the evil doings of God's creations—including the unforgiveable evil of belonging to the wrong religion.

Religions could, of course, have simply announced that their doctrine of the need for "perfection" and "justice" in heaven arose out of a misunderstanding of the true nature of God, but then there would be no need for judgment, condemnation, and punishment in the afterlife—and that frightening prospect is the chief tool of member recruitment and member retention for most religions.

Thus it has been repeatedly declared through centuries and millennia that heaven can only accept the perfect and the just—and so, the need for the *mildly* imperfect to be purified (through suffering in Purgatory) and the *unforgivably imperfect* to be purged (through everlasting punishment in hell) has been firmly cemented in humanity's religious teachings, both in the past and, archaic as those teachings may seem, to this very day.

☀

Let's look now at what is really true about all of this.

No amount of continuing explanatory narrative on this subject can come close to the clarity of a single passage from the original material supporting the text you are holding in your hand, so let's go there for some clarity.

Following is an excerpt from the *CwG* book, *The New Revelations.* As you may know, this is a conversation between God and humanity.

God speaks first.

> Even if I did hold the extraordinarily unGodly thought that you did not "deserve" heaven, why would I have a need to seek some kind of revenge, or punishment, for your failing? Wouldn't it be a simple matter for Me to just dispose of you? What vengeful part of Me would require that I subject you to eternal suffering of a type and at a level beyond description?
>
> If you answer, "The need for justice," would not a simple denial of communion with Me in heaven serve the ends of justice? Is the unending infliction of pain also required?
>
> I tell you there is no such experience after death as you have constructed in your fear-based theologies. Yet there is an experience of the soul so unhappy, so incomplete, so less than whole, so separated from God's greatest joy, that to your soul this would be hell.
>
> But I tell you I do not send you there, nor do I cause this experience to be visited upon you. You, yourself, create the experience, whenever and however you separate your Self from your own highest thought about you.
>
> You, yourself, create the experience, whenever you deny your Self; whenever you reject Who and What You Really Are.

Yet even this experience is never eternal. It cannot be, for it is not My plan that you shall be separated from Me forever and ever. Indeed, such a thing is an impossibility—for to achieve such an event, not only would you have to deny Who You Are—I would have to as well. This I will never do. And so long as one of us holds the truth about you, the truth about you shall ultimately prevail.

But if there is no hell, does that mean I can do what I want, act as I wish, commit any act, without fear of retribution?

Is it fear that you need in order to be, do, and have what is intrinsically right? Must you be threatened in order to "be good"? And what is "being good"? Who gets to have the final say about that? Who sets the guidelines? Who makes the rules?

I tell you this: You are your own rule-maker. You set the guidelines. And you decide how well you have done; how well you are doing. For you are the one who has decided Who and What You Really Are—and Who You Want to Be. And you are the only one who can assess how well you're doing.

No one else will judge you ever, for why, and how, could God judge God's own creation and call it bad? If I wanted you to be and do everything perfectly, I would have left you in the state of total perfection whence you came. The whole point of the process was for you to discover yourself, create your Self, as you truly are—and as you truly wish to be. Yet you could not be that unless you also had a choice to be something else.

Should I therefore punish you for making a choice that I Myself have laid before you? If I did not want you to make the second choice, why would I create other than the first?

This is a question you must ask yourself before you would assign Me the role of a condemning God.

The direct answer to your question is, yes, you may do as you wish without fear of retribution. It may serve you, however, to be aware of consequences.

Consequences are results. Natural outcomes. These are not at all the same as retributions, or punishments. Outcomes are simply that. They are what results from the natural application of natural laws. They are that which occurs, quite predictably, as a consequence of what *has* occurred.

All physical life functions in accordance with natural laws. Once you remember these laws, and apply them, you have mastered life at the physical level.

What seems like punishment to you—or what you would call evil, or bad luck—is nothing more than a natural law asserting itself.

A lot of people don't "get" this idea of a God Who says, "There's no such thing as right and wrong," and, Who proclaims that we will never be judged.

Well, make up your mind! First you say I'm judging you, then you're upset because I'm not.

I know, I know. It's all very confusing. We're all very . . . complex. We don't want Your judgments, but we do. We don't want Your punishments, yet we feel lost without them.

And when You say . . . "I will never punish you," we cannot believe that—and some of us almost get mad about that. Because if You're not going to judge and punish us, what will keep us walking the straight and narrow? And if there's no "justice" in heaven, who will undo all the injustice on the earth?

Why are you counting on heaven to correct what you call "injustice"? Do not the rains fall from the heavens?

Yes.

And I tell you this: The rain falls on the just and the unjust alike.

But what about, "Vengeance is Mine, sayeth the Lord"?

I never said that. One of you made that up, and the rest of you believed it.

"Justice" is not something you experience after you act a certain way, but *because* you act a certain way. Justice is an act, not punishment *for* an act.

I see that the problem with our society is that we seek "justice" after an "injustice" has occurred, rather than "doing justice" in the first place.

Right on the head! You've hit the nail right on the head! Justice is an action, not a reaction. Do not, therefore, look to Me to somehow "fix everything in the end" by imposing some form of celestial justice in the "afterlife."

I tell you this: There is no "afterlife," but only life. Death does not exist. And the way you experience and create your life, as individuals and as a society, is your demonstration of what you think is just.

And Two More Things, Please

We also touched here on two other topics that we promised to expand on a bit before this narrative was complete.

You may recall that in Chapter 9 it was said: "God is life itself, which is the expression of love in physical form. Every expression of life is an expression of love. It may not appear that way through the eyes of limited perception, but it is surely, profoundly, and eternally true."

That deserves explanation.

Every act is an act of love. Some acts of love are deeply distorted, terribly maligned, and what we would all call horribly evil, yet they are birthed by love and expressions of love—however deformed or disfigured they may be.

If a person loves nothing, that person will hate nothing. For a person only hates if a person cannot have something that a person loves, or if that which a person loves is taken away.

If a person loves nothing, that person will never be angry. For a person is angry only if something that a person loves is violated, obstructed, denied, or damaged in some way.

The one who does not love simply does not care.

This does not mean that horrible, ugly acts by human beings are in any way condoned. But they can be understood.

The challenge facing humanity is that, still at its near-infant stage, it has not yet learned how to love in every case without ever doing damage. It is possible for highly evolved beings to exist in this way. Very few human beings have reached the level of consciousness and awareness from which such behavior would inevitably and always emerge.

God knows this, and God understands.

The remarkable insight that every act is an act of love can be applied to our response when others do things that we feel hurt or damage us in some way. The quickest way to use it is to immediately, when feeling hurt or damaged, think of a time when we might have done the same thing, or nearly the same thing in content if not in degree, in our own dealings with another.

There are very few offenses that have been committed against us that we have not committed, at least in some form. Every spiritual tradition recognizes this. That is why we have been given such wonderful tools as statements like these:

> "Let those who are without sin among you cast the first stone."
>
> "Judge not, that ye yourself not be judged."
>
> "Forgive us our trespasses, as we forgive those who trespass against us."

The wisdom here is far deeper than might originally have been thought. It is rooted in the knowledge that all acts are acts of love, and that we, ourselves, would never have hurt another, deliberately or otherwise, had we ourselves not loved something so deeply that we acted out in ways that were injurious to others.

It is not natural for human beings to hurt other human beings. It is simply not part of our *nature*. It has been said that only the injured injure. And that is true. Which is why one of the most reparative, restorative, remedial things we could ever say to someone who we experience having damaged us is: "Please tell me . . . what hurts you so much that you feel you have to hurt me in order to heal it?"

The second thing we touched on in the text above was found in Chapter 18, where it was said that all self-service is service to the Whole. "There are multiple reasons this is true, as will become apparent before this narrative is concluded," it said there, and I hope by now this is so—particular after your having read Chapter 23.

There, as you will remember, it said: "All things are One Thing. There is only One Thing, and all things are part of the One Thing there is."

This means a great deal more than "you are your brother's keeper." This means that you *are* your brother, and your brother is you; that there is no separation, but only the appearance of separation, between you and God and between you and any other living thing.

How I have internalized this is with a simple statement: What I do for you, I do for me. What I fail to do for you, I fail to do for me. There's only one of us. I know it looks as if there's more than one of us, but we are a single being, individuated. And we all desire the same thing, because we all *are* the same thing: Love. We are simply seeking to express and experience Who We Are.

The Moment of Choice is Here

THE TIME HAS COME to make a decision. Not because you're nearing the end of this book, but because humanity as a collective is nearing the end of its ability to go on the way it has been.

That isn't meant to be a doomsday warning, just a word to the wise. We have to change course here, and the fastest way we can do it is to change our ideas about God.

That's the decision we're now being invited to make. Are we ready to change our mind about God? And while we're at it, are we ready to make a firm and final decision about ourselves and about who we are?

With nearly five billion of the world's seven billion people professing a belief in a higher power, you can bet your life (in fact, you *are*) that important decisions are being made—political decisions, economic decisions, environmental decisions, educational decisions, social decisions, and spiritual decisions—based on *what* people believe *about* this higher power. That includes you.

So this business of how humanity thinks about God, and how human beings think of themselves in relationship to God, is no small matter—a point we made in the first sentence of the first chapter of this book.

For instance, think of the lives that would be saved if our species simply dropped all behaviors that arose from the notion that we are all separated from each other and from God.

Imagine how life would be on this planet if we simply acted as if there is no separation between us—that it really is *true* that what I do for you, I do for me, and what I fail to do for you, I fail to do for me. The political, economic, and social ramifications of that single idea are staggering. With the on-the-ground implementation of such a thought, all of the systems we have created to produce a better life for everyone could actually *work*.

Finally.

Starvation could end. Oppression could end. Domination could end. Terrorism could end. Despoiling of the environment could end. Abject poverty could end. Worldwide human suffering could end.

Our dysfunctional behaviors *can't* end now because they are based on, and emerge from, a "survival of the fittest" mentality that only a belief in separation could produce. And in every civilization where the highest value is survival of the Whole rather than survival of its parts, a huge transformation takes place.

This can happen now on the earth.

Not overnight. No. Not in a week or a month or a year. No. But sooner rather than later? Yes. In decades rather than centuries? Yes. Because our collective consciousness of oneness will rapidly override and render undesirable all of our previous unconscionable behaviors.

Yet this is not a matter of only global consequence. Changing your mind about your oneness with God and with each other can have immediate and remarkable implications in your own life.

More peace can be yours. More joy can be yours. Greater sufficiency can be yours. More love and companionship can be yours. And not just temporarily. Not just once in a while. Not just now and then, but all through the rest of your life. And all from a simple shift in your thinking.

This text is intended to get you started in that direction. It ends here with an invitation for you to start here. It challenges you to make a simple choice. That choice has to do with how you see yourself in the universe.

I wrote about this in *The Storm Before the Calm*, and I want to repeat here what I said there, because the following single decision could change your life forever.

Proposition: You (and all of us) have two choices when it comes to how you think of yourself.

Choice #1: You could conceive of yourself as a chemical creature, a "logical biological incident." That is, the logical outcome of a biological process engaged in by two older biological processes called your mother and your father.

If you see yourself as a chemical creature, you would see yourself as having no more connection to the larger processes of life than any other chemical or biological life form.

Like all the others, you would be impacted *by* life, but could have very little impact *on* life. You certainly couldn't create events, except in the most remote, indirect sense. You could create more *life* (all chemical creatures carry the biological capacity to recreate more of themselves), but you could not create what life *does*, or how it "shows up" in any given moment.

Further, as a chemical creature you would see yourself as having very limited ability to create an intentioned *response* to the events and conditions of life. You would see yourself as a creature of habit and instinct, with only those resources that your biology brings you.

You would see yourself as having more resources than a turtle, because your biology has gifted you with more. You would see yourself as having more resources than a butterfly, because your biology has gifted you with more.

You would see yourself as having more resources than an ape or a dolphin (but, in those cases, perhaps not all that *many* more), because your biology has gifted you with more. Yet that is all you would see yourself as having in terms of resources.

You would see yourself as having to deal with life day-by-day pretty much as it comes, with perhaps a tiny bit of what seems like "control" based on advance planning, etc., but you would know that at any minute anything could go wrong—and often does.

Choice #2: You could conceive of yourself as a spiritual being inhabiting a biological mass—what I call a "body."

If you saw yourself as a spiritual being, you would see yourself as having powers and abilities far beyond those of a simple chemical creature; powers that transcend basic physicality and its laws.

You would understand that these powers and abilities give you collaborative control over the *exterior* elements of your individual and collective life and complete control over the *interior* elements—which means that you have total ability to create your own reality, because your reality has nothing to do with *producing* the exterior elements of your life and everything to do with how you *respond to* the elements that have been produced.

Also, as a spiritual being, you would know that you are here (on the earth, that is) for a spiritual reason. This is a highly focused purpose and has little to do directly with your occupation or career, your income or possessions or achievements or place in society, or *any* of the exterior conditions or circumstances of your life.

You would know that your purpose has to do with your *interior* life—and that how well you do in *achieving* your purpose may very often have an *effect* on your exterior life.

(For the interior life of each individual cumulatively produces the exterior life of the collective. That is, those people around you, and those people who are around those people who are around you. It is in this way that you, as a spiritual being, participate in the evolution of your species.)

My own answer: I've decided that I am a spiritual being, a three-part being made up of body, mind, and soul. Each part of my tri-part being has a function and a purpose. As I come to understand each of those functions, each aspect of me begins to more efficiently serve its purpose in my life.

I am an Individuation of Divinity, an expression of God, a singularization of the singularity. There is no separation between me and God, nor is there any difference, except as to proportion. Put simply, God and I are one.

This brings up an interesting question. Am I rightly accused of heresy? Are people who believe that they are divine nothing but raving lunatics? Are they, worse yet, apostates?

I wondered. So I did a little research. I wanted to find out what religious and spiritual sources had to say on the subject. Here's some of what I found . . . .

> Isaiah 41:23—*Shew the things that are to come hereafter, that we may know that ye are gods: yea, do good, or do evil, that we may be dismayed, and behold together.*

Psalm 82:6—*I have said, 'Gods ye are, And sons of the Most High—all of you.*

John 10:34—*Jesus answered them, Is it not written in your law, "I said, Ye are gods?"*

The Indian philosopher Adi Shankara (788 CE – 820 CE), the one largely responsible for the initial expounding and consolidation of Advaita Vedanta, wrote in his famous work, *Vivekachudamani*: *"Brahman is the only Truth, the spatio-temporal world is an illusion, and there is ultimately Brahman and individual self."*

Sri Swami Krishnananda Saraswati Maharaj (April 25, 1922 – November 23, 2001), a Hindu saint: "*God exists; there is only one God; the essence of man is God.*"

According to Buddhism there ultimately is no such thing as a Self that is independent from the rest of the universe (the doctrine of *anatta*). Also, if I understand certain Buddhist schools of thought correctly, humans return to the earth in subsequent lifetimes in one of six forms, the last of which are called Devas . . . which is variously translated as *Gods* or *Deities*.

Meanwhile, the ancient Chinese discipline of Taoism speaks of embodiment and pragmatism, engaging practice to *actualize the Natural Order within themselves.* Taoists believe that man is a microcosm for the universe.

Hermeticism is a set of philosophical and religious beliefs or gnosis based primarily upon the Hellenistic Egyptian pseudepigraphical writings attributed to Hermes Trismegistus. Hermeticism teaches that there is a transcendent God, The All, or one "Cause," of which we, and the entire universe, participate.

The concept was first laid out in *The Emerald Tablet of Hermes Trismegistus*, in the famous words: *"That which is Below corresponds to that which is Above, and that which is*

Above, corresponds to that which is Below, to accomplish the miracles of the One Thing."

And in Sufism, an esoteric form of Islam, the teaching, *There is no God but God* was long ago changed to, *There is nothing but God.* Which would make me . . . well . . . *God.*

*

Enough? Do you wish or need more? You might find it instructive and fascinating to go to Wikipedia, the source to which I owe my appreciation for much of the above information.

As well, read the remarkable books of Huston Smith, a globally honored professor of religion. Among titles of his that I most often recommend: *The World's Religions: Our Great Wisdom Traditions* (1958, revised edition 1991, HarperOne), and *Forgotten Truth: The Common Vision of the World's Religions* (1976, reprint edition 1992, HarperOne).

So . . . that is my response to the invitation that life is presenting me, and all of us, regarding the making of a choice about Who I Am. I am an out-picturing of The Divine. I am God in human form. As are we all.

What is your response?

Putting It All Together: A Simple Statement Explaining Everything

A LOT HAS BEEN said in this book. I hope that it has helped you. I know from its title that you would not have picked it up if you were not creating in your life as many opportunities as you possibly can to continue the search.

I don't even have to tell you what search I'm talking about. You know exactly what I mean.

If *God's Message to the World* has moved you forward on that search by leading you to a closer awareness of your own truth, it has done what it set out to do. Even if your truth is diametrically opposed to what has been said here, this book has done its job. For its purpose from the very beginning, as *stated* in the very beginning, is not to convince you of anything, but to propose to you some ideas that might be worth exploring.

I'm going to ask your permission to conclude this text by summarizing this entire book in thirty-five paragraphs. Your kind permission is requested because in order for me to do this, I must once again use a tool that I have used liberally throughout: Repetition.

As I said very early on, our Ancient Cultural Story has hung on for so long for the very reason that its espousers have had no qualms or uneasiness about repeating it over and over again.

This book suggests in something like 60,000 words across twenty-six chapters that we write a New Cultural Story to replace the old, creating a new way to be human to replace the old, producing a new experience of life to replace the old.

Now here is the simple, direct statement that humanity has been waiting for, a clear, concise explanation of the entirety of the Human Experience:

THE DIVINE PURPOSE IS for life to be used by Divinity to express divinity in order that Divinity may experience divinity in all of its aspects. In short, God is using life in order to experience Itself.

Divinity can be experienced only through the expression of it. Divinity can be imagined, it can be thought about, and it can be held in awareness by the soul, but until it is expressed, it is merely a concept; unless it is expressed, it cannot be experienced.

Here, then, is the soul's knowing: Until you express divinity you cannot experience divinity.

You can talk about love, you can imagine love, you can think about love, you can hold love as an idea conceptually, but until you express it, you cannot experience it.

You can talk about compassion, you can imagine compassion, you can think about compassion, you can hold compassion as an idea conceptually, but until you express it, you cannot experience it.

You can talk about understanding, you can imagine understanding, you can think about understanding, you can hold understanding as an idea conceptually, but until you express it, you cannot experience it.

Divinity is all of these things, and much more. It is patience and kindness, goodness and mercy, acceptance and forbearance, wisdom and clarity, gentleness and beauty, selflessness and nobility, benevolence and generosity. And yes, much more than even that.

You can imagine all of these things, you can think about all of these things, you can hold all of these things as ideas conceptually, but until you express all of these things in you, through you, as you, you have not experienced divinity.

And you will never have an opportunity to experience these things unless life provides you with such an opportunity. This is what life is doing every day. Indeed, this is the purpose of life itself.

Therefore, when life brings you challenges, difficulties, and unique conditions, situations, and circumstances that are ideally suited to bring out the best in you, "judge not, and neither condemn," but be a light unto the darkness, that you might know Who You Really Are—and that all those whose lives you touch might know who they are as well, by the light of your example.

While the idea that "God uses life to know God Self" is surely not new, why God works this way may very well be something you'd like to know more about. So here is the explanation.

God cannot experience all that God is within the spiritual realm alone, because in that realm there is nothing that God is not. The realm of the spiritual is the place where God is all there is, where love is all there is, where perfection is all there is. It's a wonderful place, because there is nothing but divinity. It is, in short, what you would call heaven.

There is, however, this particular reality: There is nothing that God is not. And in the absence of what God is not, what God is . . . is not able to be experienced.

The same is true about you. You cannot experience what you are except in the presence of what you are not. Nor is anything able to be experienced unless it is in a contextual field that includes its opposite.

The light cannot be experienced without the darkness. "Up" has no meaning in experience without "down." "Fast" is simply a term, a word having no meaning whatsoever without "slow."

Only in the presence of the thing called "small" can the thing called "big" be experienced. We can say that something is "big," we can imagine that something is "big," we can conceptualize something as being "big," but in the absence of something that is "small," "big" cannot be experienced.

Likewise, in the absence of something "finite," "infinity" cannot be experienced. Put into theological terms, we can know "divinity" conceptually, but we cannot know it experientially.

Therefore, all the people and events of your life—now or in the past—which seem to be "at odds" with who you are and what you choose to experience, are simply gifts from the highest source, created for you and brought to you through the collaborative process of co-creating souls, allowing you to find yourself in a contextual field within which the fullest experience of Who You Really Are becomes possible.

Or, as it was so wonderfully stated in *Conversations with God:* "I have sent you nothing but angels."

Now there's a statement to remember. It was said here that your eternal sacred journey has a purpose, and it does indeed. It is a purpose established by divinity Itself.

The divine purpose is to expand the Reality of God.

Em Claire crystalizes this idea for us with her poem, *What Is It That You Were Given?*

What is it that you were given?
I mean from the loss.
After
what was taken.
That very thing you could never live without:
the person
or place;
secret or circumstance.
Now that It is gone
and you can no longer call It foundation—

what is it that you were given?

You know, and I know this:
there is a hollowing out.
Something comes and opens you up

right
down
the
middle

And from that moment on
you are no longer immune to this world.

You wake, you wander—
every familiar now a foreign.
You walk as through water
until you make it back to your bed
and finally, even there, your sheets,
your own pillow's scent—different—
as if daily someone repaints your room,
displaces something;
disturbs a cherished memento.

You see, sometimes we *are* emptied.

We are emptied because Life wants us to know

so
much
more

Light.

In simple terms (and these are simple terms), God is growing—becoming more of Itself—through the process called life. God IS this process. God is both the process of life itself . . . and the result of it. Thus, God is the Creator and the Created. The Alpha and the Omega. The Beginning and the End. The Unmoved Mover. The Unwatched Watcher.

In not so simple terms, God cannot "grow" because everything that God ever was, is now, or ever will be, *is Now*. There is no time and there is no space. Therefore, there is no time in which to grow, and no space into which to grow. The cycle of life is occurring simultaneously everywhere.

What the human mind wants to call God's "growth" is the process by which Individuations of Divinity experience, and thus become aware of, more and more of what God already knows Itself to be. Yet even this would seem to require the sensation or condition called "time" in order to occur . . . unless . . . all the content of life is, in Ultimate Reality, manifest all at once in a single place—even as, on the DVD of a movie, the entire story exists in its totality right now, yet we experience the story *unfolding* by simply looking at the totality in a particular way. This process by which God causes Its individual parts to experience the Whole piece-by-piece is what has loosely been called evolution.

Not all of this is easily or completely explained in human terms. No finite form, by the very reason of it being finite, could hold the infinite consciousness, awareness, and experience of the Whole, yet each individuated form was designed uniquely to reflect a particular aspect of divinity Itself, with the Whole dividing Itself (not to be confused with separating Itself) from Itself, re-creating Itself in smaller and finite form.

Putting all these aspects together again, as one puts the pieces of a puzzle together, produces a picture of what all the pieces create. Namely: God.

All the pieces are part of the picture, and no piece is less a part of the picture than any other.

Now some forms of life have been endowed with a level of Essential Essence (the raw energy from which everything springs) sufficient to produce the possibility of that Essence knowing Itself. This is the quality in certain living things that is called Self-Consciousness.

Human life (and, we suspect with good reason, life elsewhere in the universe) was designed in such a way that what we call "expansion" of consciousness and experience is possible.

In fact, human consciousness can expand even to a point where it once again knows itself as part of The Whole. Jesus, for instance, said: "I and the Father are one." He understood his relationship to God perfectly. He understood that the picture which the puzzle created was not complete without him. He was the completion. As are we all.

Take one piece of the puzzle away and the picture is not complete. The experience of becoming fully self-conscious occurs through a process by which the individuated aspect does not grow, actually, but simply becomes more and more aware that it does not have to grow, but truly is, in its individuated form, divinity Itself. The individual piece recognizes itself as the puzzle itself, simply divided.

The spectacular physiological, psychological, and theological transition into that higher level of self-awareness occurs only once in the epochal history of every sentient species in the cosmos—and this is precisely what is happening within the human race right now.

Is This Really a Message from God?

As surely as anything in life is a message from The Divine (and much of it has been declared by many to be exactly that), the ideas in this book are also. You brought them to yourself, drawing them into your sphere as certainly as you have at some level magnetized everything in your experience, and all for the same purpose: your own evolution.

God has placed the messages found here before the world prior to this moment. Many, many times have these messages been sent. Through all the years and all the ages of humanity have these truths been made known, in the voices and in the writings of countless people.

And now, the day of the individual messenger is over. This is the moment in our history when the cumulative message of all of humanity is displaying its cumulative effect in fullness. Because now, for the first time in the experience of our species, *we can all talk to each other instantly.*

The Internet in this moment has done for humanity what Gutenberg's printing press did in 1440. That method of printing not only created a revolution in the production of books, but also pushed the evolution of an entire species forward at triple speed by making it practical to *spread knowledge* and *share wisdom* through the making of texts—and the information they carried—widely available.

Then, just when we'd thought we'd reached the height of information transferability by the middle of the twentieth century, along came the Internet, doing precisely the same thing now that the printing press did 500 years ago, but this time lurching humanity's evolution forward at *quintuple* speed.

And just as there were mighty efforts to stop the masses from being opened to certain ideas by banning certain books (a practice that continues to this day), so, too, are there now gargantuan efforts in some countries to ban certain websites, and in many more nations to limit the overall reach of the Internet itself, for everyone—and all toward the same end: So that certain ideas—ideas that those in control, those in positions of power, do not want shared—cannot be easily or quickly spread.

Yet the forward movement of evolution will not, and cannot, be stifled, only slightly slowed—and the day will come when the sharing of revolutionary ideas about God will create a Whole New Cultural Story for humanity.

☀

I tell you, the day will yet come when we will wonder how we could ever have thought that we and God were not One; how we could ever have thought that we and every other human being in every other country did not hold the exact same interest, and was not due the same *share,* in all the wealth, resources, and wonder that is available in physical life on this glorious planet.

The day will yet come when we will wonder how we could ever have thought that God had "chosen ones" who were better than any other of God's people, that men were better than women, that whites were better than blacks, that straights were better than gays—or that the *idea* of "better" even *existed* in the mind of God.

For this day to come sooner rather than later, we are going to have to shift our emphasis on how to solve humanity's problems. To be fair to our species, it is not as if we have not tried. We have. But the difficulty—the reason that billions upon billions still live in abject poverty, without even electricity or the dignity of indoor sanitation—is that humanity has for centuries tried to solve its problems *at every level except the level at which the problems exist.*

It continues to do so today.

We approach our problems today as if they were political problems, open to political solutions. We talk about them, we hold debates about them, we pass resolutions about them.

When nothing changes, we seek to solve our problems through economic means. We throw money at them, or withhold money from them, as in the case of sanctions.

When that fails we say, "Aha! This is a problem to give to the military. We'll solve it with force." So we shoot bullets at it and drop bombs on it. That never works, either, if a long-term solution is what anyone is looking for. But do you think we would learn?

No. We just start the cycle all over again. So we call for "peace talks" and return to the negotiating table. There, we negotiate reparations and financial aid to heal the open wounds and quell the teeming masses. When that proves to be only a stopgap, we're at it again. Bring out the guns. Bring in the body bags.

The reason we keep running like a mouse on a wheel is that no one dares to look at the *cause* of the ongoing condition we seemed fated to endure.

Either we truly don't know, or we're afraid to admit, that our biggest problem today is not a political problem, it's not an economic problem, and it's not a military problem.

The problem facing humanity today is a spiritual problem. It has to do with humanity's *beliefs*.

Once this is understood, the solution becomes obvious. Until it's understood, the solution escapes everyone.

I observe that most people construct their lives around two responses: thinking and doing. They think about things, and they do things; think about things and do things; think about things and do things. And what they do *depends on what they think*.

This may seem almost absurdly obvious, yet it is important to say here nonetheless, because nearly every one of the planet's nonprofit organizations and governmental agencies are seeking to better our world by changing what humans are doing rather than what humans are thinking.

It's what people *believe* that creates their behavior. We have said this here over and over again, and it can't be said often enough. It is at the level of belief, not at the level of behavior, where humanity's experience will be most profoundly modified.

For decades we've been talking in psychology circles about *behavior modification*, or Behavior Mod. What we really should be talking about is Belief Mod. Yet we're talking now about the most sacred part of people's underpinnings. Many people would rather die for their beliefs—or kill others—than change them.

It doesn't matter whether the beliefs themselves are functional. It doesn't matter whether they are making people happy and producing a better life. Some people would rather be unhappy doing what they believe, than happy doing something else.

This is the crux of the problem. This is where the human family must now focus all of its attention. If we really want to change our own lives and, in the wonderful words of Robert Kennedy, seek a newer world, *this is where we must now focus all of our attention.*

Consider this final excerpt from *The New Revelations*:

> All behaviors are sponsored by beliefs.
>
> You cannot make a long-term change in behaviors without addressing the beliefs that underlie them.
>
> Your world is facing enormous problems right now, and you must *solve the problems at the level of belief.* You cannot solve the problems at the level of behavior.
>
> Seek to change beliefs, not behaviors.
>
> After you change a belief, the behavior will change by itself.

But we are a very action-oriented society. The Western world, in particular, has always found it solutions in action, not in quiet contemplation or philosophy.

> You can take whatever action you want to take to alter someone else's behavior or to stop it, but unless you alter the beliefs that produced such behavior, you will alter nothing and stop nothing. You can alter a belief in two ways. Either by enlarging upon it, or by changing it completely. But you must do one or the other or you will not alter behavior. You will merely interrupt it.

In other words, the behavior will return.

> Is there any question about that? Do you not see your history repeating itself?

I see that, yes. And it's frustrating.

Your species does the same thing over and over again because your species has not changed its basic beliefs—about God and about Life—*in millennia.*

Beliefs are taught in virtually every school on your planet, in nearly every culture, in one form or another. Often you present beliefs as "facts," but they are beliefs nonetheless.

This would not be so bad, and would not produce such terrible results, if what you believe, if what you taught, was what is so. But it is *not* what is so. You teach your children what is *not* so, and *tell them* "this is what's so."

For the most part you are not doing this intentionally. You do not know that these are falsehoods. They are, after all, the things that *you* were taught. You thus assume them to be true. It is in this way that the "sins of the father are visited upon the son, even unto the seventh generation."

In some schools—particularly some religious schools where children in their earliest years are encouraged to view life through the prism of particular religious doctrines and cultural prejudices—the result of this is the inbreeding of incredibly negative behaviors reflecting extraordinarily mistaken beliefs.

You teach your children to believe in an intolerant God, and thus condone for them their own behaviors of intolerance.

You teach your children to believe in an angry God, and thus condone for them their own behaviors of anger.

You teach your children to believe in a vengeful God, and thus condone for them their own behaviors of vengeance.

> Then you send these, your children, to do battle with the demons of your own creation. It is not an accident that by far the highest numbers of "warriors" in any radical movement are the young.
>
> When you move the youngest among you from religious schools or military academies directly into your fighting forces, promising them that they are struggling for "a higher cause" or "a grander purpose" or that *God is on their side*, what are they to think?
>
> Are they to contradict their elders, their teachers, their priests, their ulama?
>
> Yet if you are not careful, *your own children will undo you.*

And so the central challenge of our time is clear: to invite, encourage, induce humanity to consider—just *consider*—the possibility that there may be something we do not fully understand about God and about life, the understanding of which would change everything.

What our world needs now is a civil rights movement for the soul, freeing humanity at last from the oppression of its beliefs in a violent, angry, and vindictive God.

To that end I have joined with those who agree with this point of view around the world to create Humanity's Team (www.HumanitysTeam.org), and through that worldwide organization to ignite an Evolution Revolution.

I invite you all to join in that effort, for the elevation of humanity through the evolution of humanity is not something that can be accomplished without you. It invites, encourages—nay, pleads for—your direct involvement.

The great sadness is that we imagine we can't change any of this. The great happiness is that we can. All it takes is a shift in consciousness—and that is easier to bring about than most people think.

All change in consciousness is created by people who have already changed their consciousness, and who then actively, excitedly, and expansively talk about their ideas with others, describing the possibilities that a New Cultural Story places before humanity.

In *The Storm Before the Calm*, I shared a sparklingly brilliant observation shared with humanity by Margaret J. Wheatley, author of *Turning to One Another: Simple Conversations to Restore Hope to the Future* (2002). Ms. Wheatley is not someone without credentials. A globally known consultant on organizational behavior, she received her doctorate from Harvard University, holds an M.A. in systems thinking from New York University, and has worked on every inhabited continent in virtually every type of organization. Here's what she says:

> "There is no more powerful way to initiate significant social change than to start a conversation."

And so you see, there is something you can do. And you do not have to turn your own life upside-down, or sign up to devote hundreds of hours a month that you do not have to spare, in order to do it. You simply need to be willing to talk about things. To say out loud what is in your heart.

You can do this by bringing the subject up whenever and wherever stimulating people congregate. You could even *cause* them to congregate by starting a discussion group in your own home. If you want to be really daring, invite the pastor of your local church to allow you to start a discussion group there.

If this seems all too "visible" for your taste, you could become what I call a "quiet activist." Offer this book to family and friends from the "for what it's worth department," and just ask them what they think of it. Accidentally leave copies of it everywhere. Forget that you placed it on a park bench or your subway seat. Add it to the reading material on the table at the hair styling salon. Misplace it at the coffee shop. Lose it on an airplane. Let it find its way to the book table at your organization's charity rummage sale. Create ways to join an underground distribution network.

If you think that openly talking about all of this might feel out of place in today's fast-paced, sorry-no-time-to-talk world, consider that Ms. Wheatley observed in a 2002 article in *Utne Reader* that ". . . true conversation is . . . a timeless and reliable way for humans to think together. Before there were classrooms, meetings, or group facilitators, there were people sitting around talking.

> "We can take courage from the fact that this is a process we all know how to do. We can also take courage in the fact that many people are longing to converse again . . . we are awakening an ancient practice, a way of being gathered that all humans intimately understand."

Having said that, Ms. Wheatley offered a powerful concluding comment:

> "Change doesn't happen from someone announcing the plan. Change begins from deep inside a system, when a few people notice something they will no longer tolerate, or when they respond to someone's dream of what's possible."

That is precisely, to the letter, what the Evolution Revolution is all about. It is a call to people everywhere, gathering in small groups of spiritual activists around the world, to ignite a global conversation that will *sow seeds of sanity*, producing at last the *civilization of Civilization*.

I invite you to the effort, for the work of the evolution of our beloved species will advance only if you see this work as truly your own.

I just pour everything into God.
I don't know if my god is
the same as your god:

Is it made of Love?
Does it want for you what *you* want for you?
Does it come to you with hands opened,
asking nothing, but ready for anything?
Does it whisper to you of Light and of
Stillness, and point you toward *any*
of the paths that will take you there?
Does it remind you of your Seeing?
Does it remind you of your Knowing?
Does it remind you of the gentlest Lover
ever you've dreamed, soothing you
all the way down the length of your body,
or caressing a weariness from your heart?

Is it ever late?
Is it ever gone?
Is it made of Love?

"Is It Made of Love?"
em claire

Additional Reading

If the message of this book has created an urge within you to continue your exploration beyond today's Cultural Story about the nature of divinity, you will find one book, in particular, extraordinarily stimulating, critically important, and hugely impactful. I have excerpted it in the present text more than once. It is titled *The New Revelations*, and it is the sixth of the *Conversations with God* volumes.

I promise you, you do not want to miss this book. And if you've read it before, read it again. It will mean even more to you now.

As well, you will find most useful the following titles, which amplify and offer considerable narrative expansion of the original material in the *Conversations with God* series:

The Only Thing That Matters
The Storm Before the Calm
The Holy Experience
When Everything Changes, Change Everything
What God Said

And if you wish to "stay connected" with the energy of this book in an interactive way, simply go to: www.CWGConnect.com, where a continuous exploration of how these messages may be applied to everyday life is undertaken daily by a growing worldwide community—and where you and I can meet and discuss all of the topics raised in this book.

About the Author

NEALE DONALD WALSCH is a modern day spiritual messenger whose work has touched the lives of millions. He has written twenty-nine books on contemporary spirituality in the twenty years since he reported having an experience in which he felt the presence of The Divine, began writing questions to God on a yellow legal pad, and received answers in a process that he describes as exactly like taking dictation. What emerged from that encounter was the nine-part *Conversations with God* series, which has been published in every major language of the world.

Mr. Walsch has told his readers and the media—which has brought global attention to his experience—that everyone is having conversations with God all the time, and that the question is not: To whom does God talk? The question is: Who listens?

He says his whole life has been changed as a result of his own decision to listen. He took notes on the questions in his heart and the answers he was receiving, so that he would always remember his exchanges with Deity. It wasn't until later that he realized he was being invited to place these words into the world, as one of many throughout history who have made their very best effort to hear and to articulate God's messages. He knows that everyone is receiving these messages, and invites all people everywhere to both share them and live them as best they can, for Neale believes the world would change overnight if only a fraction of its people embraced God's most important message of all: *You've got me all wrong.*

Books by Em Claire:

Silent Sacred Holy Deepening Heart

Home Remembers Me: Medicine Poems from Em Claire

Additional Titles by Rainbow Ridge:

Read more about them at *www.rainbowridgebooks.com*.

Consciousness: Bridging the Gap between Conventional Science and the New Super Science of Quantum Mechanics
by Eva Herr

Dying to Know You: Proof of God in the Near-Death Experience
by P. M. H. Atwater

The Cosmic Internet: Explanations from the Other Side
by Frank DeMarco

Dance of the Electric Hummingbird
by Patricia Walker

Messiah's Handbook: Reminders for the Advanced Soul
by Richard Bach

When the Horses Whisper
by Rosalyn Berne

Channeling Harrison
by David Young

God Within
by Patti Conklin

Lessons in Courage
by Bonnie Glass-Coffin and Don Oscar Miro-Quesada

Liquid Luck: The Good Fortune Handbook
by Joe Gallenberger

Imagine Yourself Well
by Frank DeMarco

What to Do When You're Dead
by Sondra Sneed

The Healing Curve
by Sara Chetkin

Rainbow Ridge Books publishes spiritual, metaphysical, and self-help titles, and is distributed by Square One Publishers in Garden City Park, New York.

To contact authors and editors, peruse our titles, and see submission guidelines, please visit our website at *www.rainbowridgebooks.com*.

For orders and catalogs, please call toll-free:
(877) 900-BOOK.